MW00412999

A WORLDWIDE TRAVEL GUIDE TO *Sea Turtles*

MARINE, MARITIME, AND COASTAL BOOKS

SPONSORED BY TEXAS A&M UNIVERSITY AT GALVESTON

WILLIAM MERRELL AND STEPHEN CURLEY, *General Editors*

A WORLDWIDE TRAVEL

TEXAS A&M UNIVERSITY PRESS ■ *College Station*

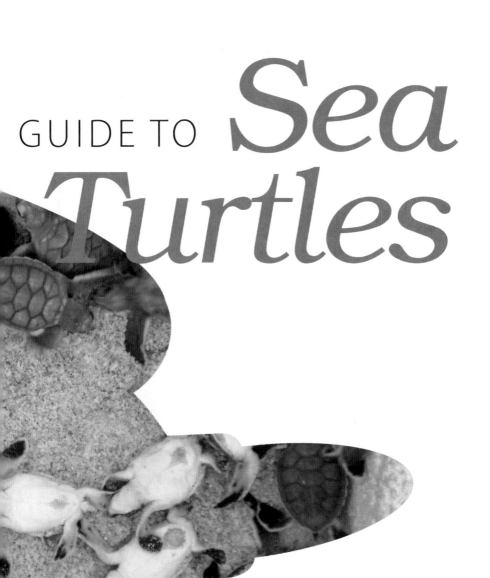

GUIDE TO *Sea Turtles*

Wallace J. Nichols
Brad Nahill
and
Melissa Gaskill

Copyright © 2014 by
Wallace J. Nichols, Brad Nahill, and Melissa Gaskill
All rights reserved
First edition

Manufactured in China by Everbest Printing Co.
through Four Colour Printing Group
This paper meets the requirements of ANSI/NISO Z39.48–1992
    (Permanence of Paper).
Binding materials have been chosen for durability.

LIBRARY OF CONGRESS CATALOGING-IN-PUBLICATION DATA

Nichols, Wallace J., author.
    A worldwide travel guide to sea turtles / Wallace J. Nichols,
Brad Nahill, and Melissa Gaskill. — First edition.
        pages cm. — (Marine, maritime, and coastal books)
    Includes index.
    ISBN 978-1-62349-161-1 (flex : alk. paper) —
    ISBN 978-1-62349-174-1 (e-book)
    1. Sea turtles—Conservation.
I. Nahill, Brad, author. II. Gaskill, Melissa, author.
III. Title. IV. Series: Marine, maritime, and coastal books.
    QL666.C536N53   2014
    597.92'8—dc23
    2013040986

Dedicated to Archie Carr,
who started the sea turtle conservation
movement; to Jairo Mora, who gave his
very life to save sea turtles; and to all the
hardworking, passionate people who walk
beaches every night for very little pay and
lots of hardship. May our children and their
children's children one day know sea turtles
simply as part of the natural world and
not as endangered species.

If we were logical, the future would be bleak indeed. But we are more than logical. We are human beings, and we have faith, and we have hope, and we can work.

—JACQUES COUSTEAU

Contents

T HIS is the inaugural volume in a series of Marine, Maritime, and Coastal Books published by Texas A&M University Press and sponsored by Texas A&M University at Galveston. The sea turtle is at the frontline of conservation efforts for endangered or threatened species, and public opinion plays a key role in helping sea turtle populations recover and remain healthy. *A Worldwide Travel Guide to Sea Turtles* is an important contribution to their continued existence. Written for both passive armchair enthusiasts and active hip-boot sloggers, it is a readable layperson's turtle-watching guide that balances the rigors of scientific accuracy with the benefits of ecotourism and volunteer vacations.

Stephen Curley and William Merrell
General Editors
Marine, Maritime & Coastal Books

A hawksbill turtle hatchling shortly after emerging from the nest in El Salvador.
(Photo by Brad Nahill/SEEtheWILD)

Preface

SEVERAL FEET below the sand, a tiny hatchling struggles out of its round, white egg. A mound of more than 100 other eggs surrounds it. One by one, other baby sea turtles begin to emerge, using a small triangular extension on their beaks to pierce the now-thin eggshells. The collapsing shells create small air spaces, and the tiny turtles thrash about. The flippers of the ones on top of the pile knock down grains of sand, which gradually build up the bottom of the nest, lifting the hatchlings like a rising tide.

Eventually, the hatchlings end up just below the surface of the beach, where they wait for cooler temperatures that signal the coming of night. Then they resume their squirming and thrashing, at last emerging from the sand into the open air. Though they have never seen or smelled the sea, the little turtles instinctively turn toward the open, lighter horizon over the water, away from the dark shadows of dunes behind them. They scramble over ridges of sand, around clumps of seaweed and driftwood, as fast as their little flippers can carry them. Some become a meal for crabs, birds, or other predators along this perilous journey.

Waves breaking on the beach briefly lift the hatchlings, which begin to swim like mad before being dropped back on the sand by the departing water. After a few tries, some succeed in remaining in the waves, which sweep them into the sea. Other predators await beneath the water, catching more of the hatchlings before they can reach the relative safety of floating mats of *Sargassum* or other shelter. Perhaps one in 1,000 hatchlings will live long enough to reach adult size, when few predators can make a meal of them, and reproduce.

This amazing phenomenon occurs by the thousands around the world, throughout the year. Those who have seen it—or the beginning of the process, a mother turtle laying her eggs—often say they will never be the same. They use words like *inspiring, transformational, remarkable.*

Perhaps you picked up this book because while snorkeling in a clear Caribbean cove, you encountered a sea turtle browsing on seagrass at the bottom. Or you saw juveniles paddling around the end of a fishing jetty or an injured or cold-stunned turtle recovering in a tank at the local aquarium. You may have been fortunate enough to watch a female haul onto a beach to nest or have seen dozens of little hatchlings scurry toward the water to face those almost insurmountable odds of survival to adulthood. Perhaps you have never seen a sea turtle at all and want to join the ranks of those who have been transformed by encounters with these ancient reptiles.

Sea turtles make excellent subjects for ecotravel. These water-dwelling reptiles are charismatic, harmless, photogenic animals that behave in predictable ways. Scientists and locals know when and where they nest and hatch and where you are likely to find them. Done right, with the safety of both sea turtle and traveler in mind, sea turtle watching becomes one of the most memorable experiences we can have with wild nature.

Responsible tourism is also a critical element in worldwide efforts to save these amazing animals (although uncontrolled tourism, ironically, can make things worse). Many sea turtle conservation, monitoring, and research programs rely on tourist visits to help fund their work, to generate local support, and even to keep poachers at bay by their very presence. By visiting and supporting the programs in this book, you can have an unforgettable encounter and will be helping to save sea turtles, their habitat, and the communities around them. Have fun, create lasting memories, and make a difference.

In this guide, we feature destinations dedicated primarily to protecting and preserving turtles and habitat, places that actively encourage visits and involve people in their activities and mission in a responsible fashion. We focus on places that are reasonably accessible and safe and that offer appropriate amenities for a pleasant and educational trip. We do not include those that exploit turtle populations or have a primary focus on tourism, or whose activities and development have negatively affected local populations or habitats.

Our goal is to direct you to places where your dollars support responsible protection efforts and local economies. In many turtle habitats, tourism can mean the difference between poaching turtle eggs and killing nesting turtles or protecting them. Sea turtle tourism can bolster local eco-industries and support the maintenance of pristine beach environments that might otherwise be developed. Tourist support of outfitters, hotels, restaurants, and guides makes it possible for locals to earn a living from turtles. Sea turtle tourism makes turtles worth more alive than dead.

Sea turtle tourism also helps people. Sea turtles nest in many developing countries, and economic hardship often bears responsibility for their decline. Ironically, these developing countries have the most to lose from continued decline in marine turtles. Research has shown that when compared to consumptive use of sea turtles, such as eating their meat or eggs or using their hides, nonconsumptive uses, such as tourism activities, generate more revenue, spread out more into local economies, create more support for management, and generate proportionally more jobs, social development, and employment opportunities for women. Maintaining these economic benefits requires restoring worldwide populations to healthy levels—an objective much less expensive to accomplish in the wild than through artificial means. Proper management and economic incentives for turtle protection, including well-designed ecotourism, are keys to that recovery. Thus, the book you hold in your hands supports better lives for people as well as sea turtles.

But again, there is much more to it than biodiversity and economics. Everyone who engages a sea turtle on land or sea remembers the experience. For many, it is a high point of the year: a moment to connect with nature, yourself, the people you are with, and the planet on which we live; to create memories that can be recalled later, bringing back the wave of good feelings and the relief from the stresses of the world around us. The cognitive benefits of interacting with sea turtles make our efforts to protect them worthwhile. Visitors and locals, children and adults, find that their lives become richer, more purposeful, and happier with the occasional sea turtle encounter.

Many destinations in this book are easily accessible and can be visited inexpensively. Some require a bit more effort or expense. But we are confident that after one sea turtle encounter, you are going to want more.

Acknowledgments

We cannot possibly thank everyone who inspired, informed, or otherwise helped us create this guide, but you know who you are. We are grateful for the input of so many working on the front lines of conservation, in policy making and research, enforcement, and ecotourism. We hope this book will in some way contribute to and support the efforts of the hundreds of dedicated people working to save and protect sea turtles around the world.

Why Sea Turtles?

1. Sea turtles live throughout the world's oceans and nest on most of its tropical and subtropical coastlines, so there are many places to see them.

2. Sea turtles are the ideal subject for conservation tourism. Many programs in a variety of locations have proven that this concept works. Where responsible sea turtle tourism programs exist, poaching stops, habitat destruction is kept at bay, and local people are better off.

3. Sea turtles are the perfect introduction to wildlife encounters, whether for accomplished outdoor enthusiasts, those completely unfamiliar with the great outdoors, or families. Sea turtles are attractive, with handsome faces and beautiful shells. They are harmless and easy to find, behave predictably, and offer extended viewing opportunities.

4. Sea turtles also make perfect subjects for wildlife photography (although not at night with a flash!). Not only do they look good but they typically do not dash away like birds or antelope. And those adorable babies!

5. Sea turtle destinations are some of the world's most beautiful places, as well as places that offer a variety of other outdoor and family activities and a lot of other wildlife—in short, places worthy of visiting in their own right. The sea turtles are icing on the cake.

6. The cognitive benefits of sea turtle encounters are unique and valuable across ages and cultures.

7. You can help sea turtles even without traveling, by supporting one of the organizations working to save and protect them and by making small changes in daily habits, such as reducing use of plastic and picking up trash anywhere in the environment (as most of it ends up in the ocean). ■

A WORLDWIDE TRAVEL GUIDE TO *Sea Turtles*

Sea Turtles and the Threats to Their Survival

EA TURTLES have changed little in the past 100 million years—appearing before and eventually outliving the dinosaurs. They swim nearly all the oceans of the world and were once so numerous that sailors reported seas literally crawling with them. Today, due to a variety of threats, six of the seven species of sea turtles are endangered or threatened. All over the world, they face challenges to their individual survival and that of their entire species, requiring unprecedented conservation efforts.

As reptiles, sea turtles breathe air but, over millennia, have evolved the ability to remain submerged for hours at a time while resting or sleeping. Their long, narrow front flippers and shorter, webbed back flippers allow them to dive to great depths and swim long distances. While some land turtles can pull their head and legs into their protective shell, sea turtles cannot. They lack teeth but have powerful jaws that crush, bite, or tear, depending on the food they eat.

Sea turtles may live for 80 or more years and can take 15 or more years to reach maturity. They spend their entire lives at sea, save the brief periods when females return to nest on the beach where they were born. Scientists are not completely sure how they find their way back, but research shows that sea turtles can orient to the earth's magnetic field, so it may play a role. As hatchlings, they likely also imprint to characteristics of the sand and water of their natal beach.

Mother sea turtles usually nest only every two or three years, but they may lay two or three nests in one year. The temperature in the nest determines the sex of the hatchlings, with warmer nests producing females and cooler nests resulting in more males. Incubation takes about six weeks to two months, and hatchlings often emerge as a group.

🐢 Sea Turtle Species

Olive Ridley *(Lepidochelys olivacea)*
IUCN vulnerable
US ESA endangered Mexico's Pacific coast, threatened all other areas

Olive ridleys are the most abundant sea turtle in the world, with perhaps 800,000 females nesting annually. They weigh 100 pounds on average as adults, with a heart-shaped carapace (top shell) about two feet in length, and one to two claws on the flippers. They eat algae, lobster, crabs, tunicates, mollusks, shrimp, and fish. The species gets its name from its olive, grayish-green color.

Olive ridley nesting has been documented in as many as 40 countries, generally June through December in the eastern Pacific. Sometimes large groups, called *arribadas* (Spanish for "arrival"), of hundreds to thousands of mother sea turtles gather offshore, then head en masse onto the beach to lay their eggs. Females also nest singly, and some do both. Theories concerning the reason for *arribada* behavior include protection from predators—the sheer numbers are simply too much for a natural predator population to eat all at once—but scientists do not know for sure why

International Union for Conservation of Nature and US ESA

The International Union for Conservation of Nature (IUCN) is the world's first and largest professional global conservation organization. On its Red List of Threatened Species, the "threatened" category includes three levels, in order of increasing threat: vulnerable, endangered, and critically endangered. Below the "threatened" category are "extinct in the wild" and "extinct." Above it are "near threatened" and "least concern." Learn more at iucnredlist.org.

The United States Endangered Species Act (US ESA) works to protect and recover imperiled species and the ecosystems on which they depend. An "endangered" species is in danger of extinction throughout all or a significant portion of its range; and a "threatened" species is likely to become a endangered within the foreseeable future. Approximately 2,095 total species have been listed. Learn more at fws.gov/endangered/laws-policies/index.html. ■

sea turtles do it. An estimated 10 million olive ridleys once nested on the Pacific coast of Mexico, but now only a single *arribada* nesting beach may remain there.

Found in tropical regions of the South Atlantic Ocean along the coasts of West Africa and South America, in the eastern Pacific Ocean along the coast from Southern California to Chile, and in the Indian Ocean, olive ridleys have suffered a 50 percent reduction in population since the 1960s.

Leatherback *(Dermochelys coriacea)*

IUCN critically endangered

US ESA endangered

The largest living marine reptile in the world at 500 to 1,500 pounds, leatherbacks can even grow as large as 2,000 pounds and more than six feet long. They are covered with a firm, leathery skin with seven lengthwise ridges, black with white, pink, and cobalt-blue highlights, with no claws on the flippers. These sea turtles can dive deeper—up to 3,000 feet—travel farther—more than 3,000 miles—and tolerate water colder than other sea turtles can. They eat jellyfish and other soft-bodied animals, and the scissorlike jaws and throat are lined with stiff spines to help them swallow such slippery prey.

Leatherbacks nest around the world, primarily now in Central America, northern South America, Trinidad, and West Africa; as well as in Indonesia; and in lesser numbers, Puerto Rico, US Virgin Islands, and southeastern Florida. According to the IUCN, the leatherback nesting population declined more than 80 percent between 1982 and 1996.

Loggerhead *(Caretta caretta)*

IUCN endangered

US ESA endangered Mediterranean Sea, North Indian Ocean, North and South Pacific Oceans; threatened northwestern Atlantic Ocean, South Atlantic Ocean, southeastern Indo-Pacific Ocean, southwestern Indian Ocean

Named for its relatively large head, an adult loggerhead weighs up to 400 pounds and measures about three feet long. Its carapace looks reddish-brown, broad near the front and tapering to a point, and creamy-yellow underneath. It has two claws on each flipper and powerful jaws to crush clams, crabs, conch, and other prey.

Nesting takes place late April to early September throughout temperate and tropical regions of the Atlantic, Pacific, and Indian Oceans. The majority of nesting occurs along the western rims of the Atlantic and Indian Oceans, with aggregations in Oman, Australia, and the United States accounting for roughly 88 percent of total nesting. Major nesting concentrations in the United States are found from North Carolina to Florida—nearly 80 percent in six Florida counties—with some nesting farther north on the East Coast and into the Gulf of Mexico to Texas. Some loggerheads nest on the island-nation of Cape Verde off the coast of Senegal and in the Mediterranean. Females lay three to five nests or more in one season and prefer narrow, steep, coarse beaches. Tagging studies have documented that Pacific populations nesting in Japan cross the entire ocean to feed on crabs along the coast of Mexico's Baja California peninsula, a developmental migration of some 15,000 miles. (See the track of a turtle named Adelita at seaturtle.org/tracking/adelita.)

Green (*Chelonia mydas*)
IUCN endangered
US ESA endangered Florida and Mexico's Pacific coast, threatened all other areas

This species weighs an average of 300 to 350 pounds as an adult, with a smooth, oval-shaped shell about 3.3 feet in length, olive-brown with darker streaks and a yellow plastron, or belly. Juveniles are omnivorous, but adult greens are the only herbivorous sea turtles, eating primarily seagrasses and algae.

Found in tropical and subtropical waters primarily between 30 degrees North and 30 degrees South latitudes, they are common around Baja California and Hawai'i, where they are referred to as black sea turtles or Pacific green sea turtles, which range from Southern California to Chile. Greens nest June to September in the southeastern United States, most of them in Florida. The largest nesting populations are found at Tortuguero on the Caribbean coast of Costa Rica and on Raine Island on Australia's Great Barrier Reef.

Hawksbill (*Eretmochelys imbricata*)
IUCN critically endangered
US ESA endangered

Weighing 100 to 200 pounds at maturity, hawksbills have a carapace about 30 inches long, with black and brown markings on a background of amber, with overlapping scutes, or scales, and a serrated rear edge. These beautiful shells, known incorrectly as tortoiseshell, are coveted for jewelry, hair decorations, and other items, and many hawksbills have been killed to support this mostly illegal trade. This species uses the raptorlike jaw for which it is named to eat sponges, which are made of tiny, glasslike needles.

They live mostly between latitudes of 30 degrees North and South in the Atlantic, Pacific, and Indian Oceans and are found in southern Florida and the Gulf of Mexico, Puerto Rico and US Virgin Islands, in the Greater and Lesser Antilles, and along the Central American mainland down to Brazil. Nesting occurs in Mexico, Costa Rica, and remote islands around Australia and in the Indian Ocean. Adult hawksbills live almost exclusively around coral reefs, except on the Pacific side of Central America, where they frequent the waters beneath mangroves.

Kemp's Ridley (*Lepidochelys kempii*)
IUCN critically endangered
US ESA endangered

The rarest and most endangered sea turtle, Kemp's ridleys are also the smallest at 85 to 100 pounds and 2.0 to 2.5 feet long. They eat crabs and other crustaceans, fish, jellyfish, and mollusks. This species lives throughout the Gulf of Mexico and along the US Atlantic seaboard from Florida to New England and occasionally shows up in the eastern Atlantic around the Azores, Morocco, and in the Mediterranean. Kemp's ridleys nest April through July in *arribadas* on one primary nesting beach in the northern Mexican state of Tamaulipas. An *arribada* of more than 40,000 ridleys was filmed in 1947, but between 1978 and 1991, only about 200 nests were recorded each year. Thanks to protection efforts, the number of nests had increased to more than 12,000 in 2006. An extensive effort also restored nesting on the Texas coast, mostly at Padre Island National Seashore, where several hundred nests have been recorded in recent years.

Flatback (*Natator depressus*)
IUCN not yet assessed, considered "vulnerable" by Australia and state of Queensland

This species, characterized by a flattened, olive-gray shell, lives only in the tropical waters of Australia and nests on remote beaches so is the least-known sea turtle. In fact, during the past few centuries, it had several names and was only formally declared a unique species in the 1980s. Adults weigh 150 to 200 pounds with a shell from 30 to 39 inches long, and they feed on jellyfish and other soft-bodied, bottom-dwelling invertebrates. The front flippers are short and smaller than those of other sea turtles about the same size.

Flatbacks appear to be abundant throughout Australian coastal waters and into the Sea of Indonesia and Gulf of Papua. Apparently, they rarely venture into deep water. Most nesting activity occurs across the northern coast of the continent, with females laying fewer but generally larger eggs than those of other sea turtle species. Nesting seasons vary from one location to another. Hatching success rate seems high, although predators such as lizards, birds, and crabs do kill hatchlings. Introduced red foxes, feral dogs, and dingos also raid nests. The Australian government protects nesting beaches and, in two of the country's largest fisheries, requires the use of special devices that allow sea turtles to escape from fishing nets.

The Nesting Experience

As you will see throughout this book, turtle walks and nest watches start once a mother sea turtle has dug a nest chamber in the sand and begun laying her eggs. Because nesting sea turtles fall into an almost trance-like state while laying their eggs, observers can get fairly close without disturbing a nesting turtle and watch the round, glistening orbs drop into the dark cavity she created in the sand. Sea turtles may lay from 80 to 120 eggs per nest. Once she is finished, the mother turtle uses her back flippers to cover the eggs with sand, then rocks her body around on the top of the nest and tosses sand with her front flippers to disguise her work. Finally, she makes a slow, labored crawl back to the water. The entire nesting process takes about 45 minutes, but the total length of a turtle walk experience usually depends on how long it takes to locate a nesting female.

SEATURTLE.ORG

Sea Turtle Identification Key

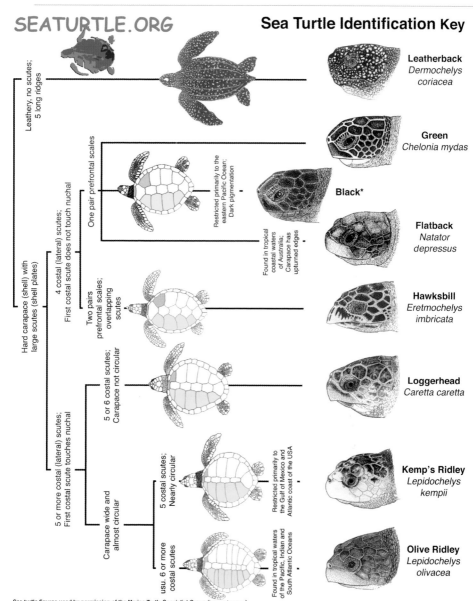

Leathery, no scutes; 5 long ridges — **Leatherback** *Dermochelys coriacea*

Hard carapace (shell) with large scutes (shell plates)

4 costal (lateral) scutes; First costal scute does not touch nuchal

One pair prefrontal scales — Restricted primarily to the eastern Pacific Ocean; Dark pigmentation — **Green** *Chelonia mydas* / **Black***

Two pairs prefrontal scales; overlapping scutes — Found in tropical coastal waters of Australia; Carapace has upturned edges — **Flatback** *Natator depressus* / **Hawksbill** *Eretmochelys imbricata*

5 or more costal (lateral) scutes; First costal scute touches nuchal

5 or 6 costal scutes; Carapace not circular — **Loggerhead** *Caretta caretta*

Carapace wide and almost circular

5 costal scutes; Nearly circular — Restricted primarily to the Gulf of Mexico and Atlantic coast of the USA — **Kemp's Ridley** *Lepidochelys kempii*

usu. 6 or more costal scutes — Found in tropical waters of the Pacific, Indian and South Atlantic Oceans — **Olive Ridley** *Lepidochelys olivacea*

Sea turtle figures used by permission of the Marine Turtle Specialist Group (iucn-mtsg.org)
Source: Pritchard, P. C. H. and Mortimer, J. A. (1999) Taxonomy, External Morphology, and Species Identification. pp. 21-38. In: Eckert, K.L., K.A. Bjorndal, F.A. Abreu-Grobois, and M. Donnelly (Editors). 1999. Research and Management Techniques for the Conservation of Sea Turtles. IUCN/SSC Marine Turtle Specialist Group Publication No. 4. (for further details see http://www.iucn-mtsg.org/publications/)   Illustrations by Tom McFarland

© seaturtle.org, used with permission

A Kemp's ridley sea turtle nesting on Padre Island National Seashore. (National Park Service, Padre Island National Seashore)

Threats to Sea Turtles

Through their exceedingly long history on earth, sea turtles have encountered many obstacles to survival—ice ages, severe storms, an extraordinary array of predators, and cataclysmic events that wiped out the dinosaurs. Yet they survived and thrived.

Until humans came along. Of course, a few indigenous people eating sea turtle meat or eggs, or catching the occasional turtle by accident on a fishing line, likely made scarcely a dent in their numbers. But as more and more people occupied the planet, that changed. Before long, sea turtle reproduction could not keep up with the rate at which humans consumed their meat and eggs. Industrial fishing efforts in much of the world's oceans began killing them in larger and larger numbers. At the same time, pollution of the ocean and beaches affected sea turtle health and survival. Nesting females encountered coastal development and obstacles on more and more beaches.

Today, sea turtles enjoy protection in many parts of the world, and the diligent efforts of scientists, conservationists, and the public have removed some of the threats to their survival. The number of sea turtles and nests have rebounded in places. The battle is far from over though. Sea turtles still face a number of daunting threats.

Fishing Activity

Our seemingly insatiable demand for inexpensive seafood represents one of the biggest threats to sea turtles. They and other wildlife are caught in trawl nets that drag behind boats for hours at a time, or on underwater hooks set on longlines, and are injured or drown. Up to a quarter of a million sea turtles get caught on hooks or ensnared in fishing lines each year, and at one time an estimated 11,000 sea turtles drowned in shrimp nets each year. That last figure decreased significantly after the United States began requiring that shrimp boats use turtle excluder devices (TEDs), a grid of bars over a flap in the net that keeps sea turtles and other larger creatures out but shrimp in. TEDs are inexpensive and effective in saving turtles about 97 percent of the time. They also reduce the bycatch of other species and, by reducing drag from larger animals in the nets, can reduce fuel consumption. The National Oceanic and Atmospheric Administration (NOAA), through its National Marine Fisheries Service, phased in requirements for shrimp boats to use TEDs and has conducted numerous workshops on their use. NOAA also has worked with other countries to develop TED programs. However, compliance remains spotty, which is a cause for concern. In recent years, for example, necropsies (animal autopsies) performed on sea turtles washed up dead on Gulf of Mexico beaches during shrimp season have revealed evidence that the turtles drowned in shrimp nets.

Most shrimp—the number-one seafood consumed in the United States—now come from farms, which often displace natural mangrove habitat and introduce chemicals into the water. If you buy shrimp, ask the seller whether it came from a farm or was wild caught, and if the latter, whether a TED was in use. If it came from a foreign shrimp farm, or was caught without the use of a TED, or if the seller does not know, do not make the purchase, and be sure the seller knows why. Let your state and federal representatives know that you support regulations that require the use of TEDs.

As many as 1.4 billion hooks may go into the oceans each year on longlines stretching for miles. Circle hooks reduce the number of sea turtles caught on these fishing lines. Circle hooks are similar to the J-shaped hooks in common use but are larger, and the hook portion points inward so that it looks like a capital *G*. This shape takes advantage of the different ways fish and sea turtles feed, making the hooks less likely to pierce a turtle's jaw. Special dehooking devices have been developed that make it easier for commercial or recreational fishers to punch a hook back out of the same hole it entered, minimizing the injury of releasing the animal.

If you go fishing, do not cast lines or set nets near turtles. If you hook or entangle a sea turtle, gently bring it close to you and lift it by its front flipper and shell, not by the hook or net. Cut the line to the hook and remove excess line, but do not remove the hook unless it is lightly set and you are certain you can do so without injuring the turtle. Keep the turtle in the shade and call local wildlife authorities, even if the turtle appears fine. It may have ingested other hooks, which will need to be removed. Never dispose of hooks and line overboard, and never place your anchor on coral or seagrass beds.

Boats, personal watercraft, and propellers also injure and kill sea turtles. Go slow in areas where sea turtles are present, and encourage others to do so.

Direct Take of Turtles and Eggs

In some places, people still covet and consume sea turtle eggs and meat. Some cultures believe sea turtle eggs have aphrodisiac properties—and, thanks to the power of the mind, if someone believes that a substance has such properties, then it does. Egg collection is particularly a problem where there are *arribadas* because so many turtles and eggs are concentrated in one place.

Sea turtles are also killed to make products from their oil, skin, and shell. Jewelry and decorative pieces made from hawksbill shells in particular remain popular, despite a ban on trade in such items under the

Convention on International Trade in Endangered Species of Wild Flora and Fauna (CITES).

Never buy items made from sea turtles. Jewelry and decorative items such as hair combs made from sea turtle shell, called tortoiseshell (although sea turtles are not tortoises), became popular in the nineteenth century. Today, items made from synthetic materials and horn can look much like tortoiseshell. While the "fake" stuff is perfectly legal to buy, it also sometimes serves as a cover for illegal trade in the real thing. An item made from actual shell commands a high price, so you likely will not find one in a typical tourist shop. But it pays to be careful so you do not inadvertently buy something made from turtle shell. Because turtle shells can be softened and shaped, items made from them appear to be all one piece, without obvious joints. A hand-carved item will bear tool marks and have tiny imperfections, while molded synthetics appear smoother. Substitute materials are painted or stained to resemble the naturally beautiful pattern of shell, and you may be able to discern whether its pattern is only surface deep. Or maybe not; substitutes have duped many. The best choice is to avoid anything touted as or resembling "tortoiseshell."

On your travels, never buy turtle eggs or meat. Express your desire to visit and support "turtle safe" communities, and voice your approval when you encounter kindred spirits. Hire local guides, visit parks and natural areas that protect nesting beaches, and patronize local businesses there. As already noted, tourism that relies on sea turtles makes the animals worth more alive than dead. When tourists come to a place specifically to see its sea turtles, locals realize that they can continuously make money from a live turtle, while they can eat or sell a dead one only once.

Artificial Lighting

At night, lights can scare away female sea turtles coming ashore to nest. If a female fails to nest after several attempts, she may resort to laying her eggs in an unsuitable place, and few if any of the hatchlings will survive. Lights draw hatchlings away from the ocean and off the beach, where they die from dehydration, exhaustion, predators, or traffic. Artificial light has been responsible for more than 50,000 hatchlings becoming disoriented in one year in Florida alone.

Fortunately, this problem is easy and inexpensive to fix. Many lights can simply be left off at night. Where light is truly needed, fixtures can be used that shield the source so light is not visible from the beach but directed downward (where it is more effective anyway). Use true red, amber, or LED bulbs, which sea turtles cannot see as well as other light bulbs.

Replace high-pressure sodium vapor lights with low-pressure ones. Apply window tint at a 15 percent transmittance level, or keep opaque curtains closed after dark. Use light only for safety, not decoration. Place security lights on motion sensors. Not only will these measures protect sea turtles but likely they will reduce energy use and costs as well: in the United States alone, an estimated one-third of all lighting, worth approximately $2 billion, is wasted in the form of sky glow and light trespass. Be sure to thank your host and others who practice turtle-friendly light management techniques.

Shoreline Armoring

The majority of the world's population lives along coastlines. When homes, resorts, and businesses are built on or near the water, inevitably storms and natural processes move and change the beach. Usually, rather than moving a structure to a more stable location, property owners do battle with nature. We build seawalls and other hard structures in hopes of stopping this natural movement and constant change. However, seawalls deflect wave energy seaward, actually worsening erosion. Unfortunately, sea turtles can not climb over these structures, although some have died trying.

Another common response to erosion, "beach renourishment," involves dredging sand from offshore or inland and spreading it onto the beach. Dredging not only destroys the benthic (bottom) community but it also stirs up sediment, choking filter feeders such as oysters and making feeding difficult for animals that find their prey by sight. It is also expensive, and most sand added to beaches washes away within five years. When sand is added to the beach during nesting season, it can actually bury sea turtle nests. The fact that the sand comes from elsewhere can also affect sea turtle nesting; mother turtles may not recognize the imported sand or find it too coarse for digging or too fine to maintain nest walls.

Seawalls can also create a false sense of security for people, serving to encourage development in unsuitable areas, leading to ever more seawalls. Ironically, natural systems such as mangroves, oyster beds, and seagrasses, which are often removed in the process of development, are all better at protecting shoreline in the first place and more hospitable to sea turtles and other marine life.

Those who own property along the coast can build responsibly, siting homes far from the high-tide line and behind dunes. Developers can leave dunes, mangroves, and grass beds in place to provide natural protection for their land and the structures on it. As much as possible, land along the shore can be left in a natural state.

Beach Trash and Water Pollution

Nearly all sea turtles that wash ashore dead or dying have plastic in their guts. Much plastic trash ultimately ends up in the ocean, where sea turtles can mistake floating plastic bags and bits of plastic—including balloons—for food. Plastic items in the ocean gradually break down into tiny particles; in some parts of the ocean, scientists have found

Plastic on a beach in El Salvador. This type of debris can be a serious problem for nesting sea turtles and hatchlings. (Photos by Michael Liles)

more of this plastic dust than natural phytoplankton and zooplankton, the tiny plants and animals that form the base of the marine food web. Small fish and other creatures eat this plastic dust and then are in turn eaten by larger fish, on up the food chain, sometimes to the plates on our tables.

Plastic debris, particularly fishing line and nets drifting just off the sea bottom, entangles turtles as they forage, often wrapping around their heads and limbs and causing serious injury. Badly entangled sea turtles can become weakened from the extra effort required to swim and feed while dragging this material and can even drown as a result.

Plastic litter, mostly discarded drink bottles, pile up on beaches around the world, even in very remote areas. Nesting sea turtles have to literally claw through this trash in order to nest, and to tiny hatchlings, piles of plastic trash may as well be the Rocky Mountains. You can help by properly disposing of all trash and minimizing the amount you create. Instead of single-use plastics, choose reusable alternatives: cloth shopping bags, metal forks and spoons, metal or glass straws (or no straw at all), recyclable paper plates or durable plastic ones designed for long-term use. Encourage others to use plastic-free or reduced plastic options, and thank your hosts when they do so.

Do not release helium balloons. These eventually burst and the pieces fall into the ocean where sea turtles can ingest them. Cigarette butts are toxic not only to sea turtles but to birds, fish, and other wildlife.

Nesting turtles and hatchlings can also get caught up in things on the beach that are not trash. Put away or consolidate beach chairs, umbrellas, coolers, and toys at night. Fill in large holes in the sand. Use permanent anchors or stands for beach umbrellas, because pushing them into the sand could destroy a nest.

Polluted water affects sea turtles by exposing them to disease and degrading or destroying their food sources. Our oceans are full of chemicals and toxins that wash from the land, including fertilizers from lawns and farms and oil from streets and driveways. Properly use fertilizers, herbicides, and pesticides or avoid their use altogether; dispose of paint and other chemicals properly; and never discard anything in creeks or other waterways, which all ultimately lead to the sea. Advocate for protections for clean water at the city, state, and federal levels. Properly maintain boats, and never dispose of anything at sea.

Climate Change

Although the earth's climate has always experienced natural variation, this natural change has been accelerated by human activity and now exceeds the ability of plants and animals to adapt. As a result, many species are likely to become extinct during the next few decades, and sea turtles are particularly vulnerable. Sea-level rise contributes to the loss of nesting habitat. Weather extremes caused by climate change mean more frequent and severe storms that cause beach erosion and that can inundate, or flood, sea turtle nests. A 2013 study revealed that sea turtle populations in the western and northeastern Indian Ocean, North and eastern Pacific Ocean, and eastern Atlantic Ocean are least likely to recover from the effects of climate change. Another study that overlaid the most active nesting beaches along the US East Coast with areas most severely affected by rising sea level found an alarming level of overlap.

Increasing beach temperature reduces hatching rates or causes complete nest failure. Temperature inside a nest determines the sex of hatchlings, with higher temperatures producing more female hatchlings. So climate change could lead to fewer hatchlings overall and shifting ratios of males to females.

Warming water temperatures in the oceans could alter current patterns, affecting the movements of migratory species such as sea turtles and changing the distribution and abundance of prey. Hotter seas cause coral bleaching, which can kill corals vital to the survival of species such as hawksbills.

The main contributors to climate change are activities that release greenhouse gases into the atmosphere, such as the burning of fossil fuels. Deforestation is also a major source of greenhouse gases. Each of us can take simple, everyday actions to help. Use energy and water more efficiently in your home and office, compost food waste, and purchase green power. Drive a fuel-efficient, low-emission vehicle; properly maintain the engine and inflate the tires; and use public transportation whenever possible. Travel typically burns fossil fuels, so look into carbon offset programs, and make every moment of your journey count. Learn more on the Environmental Protection Agency's climate change website: epa.gov/climatechange/wycd/.

Other Threats

Some of the problems of coastal development, such as seawalls and light and water pollution, have already been discussed. Some effects are more indirect, and surprising. In urban areas, populations of raccoons have increased beyond what would be supported in the wild. These animals thrive by eating pet food left outside and household garbage, and even being fed by well-meaning humans. Each year in Florida alone, raccoons destroy tens of thousands of sea turtle eggs and hatchlings. In many places, it is against the law to feed wild animals, but even if it is not illegal, it is unwise. If you live or stay near the coast, do not feed raccoons, keep garbage secure, and do not leave pet food out at night.

Feral dogs and cats can prey on sea turtle nests. Support efforts to control stray animals in your community.

Driving on the beach can compact sand, making it difficult for mother sea turtles to nest, or crushing eggs. Vehicles can also strike and kill or injure sea turtles. Deep ruts and tire tracks represent significant obstacles to little hatchlings trying to reach the sea, prolonging their journey, which can exhaust them and make them more vulnerable to predators.

Green sea turtle. (Photo by Bethany Resnick)

Motorized vehicles and beaches are not a good mix, so avoid driving on the sand except in case of emergency.

Most, if not all, of these threats can and are being addressed by various conservation and protection programs. Many people have dedicated their lives to bringing back healthy sea turtle populations—and you can help by traveling to or volunteering with these projects or simply by making relatively minor changes to your everyday behavior. Working together, let us save the sea turtles.

SEEtheWILD's Turtle-Watching Tips

1. Visit a destination that contributes positively to sea turtle conservation—including those in this book!

2. Clear beaches and water of litter, even when it is not yours.

3. Avoid single-use plastics. Much of this trash ends up in the ocean, where turtles often confuse it with food (98 percent of stranded turtles have plastic in their guts). Helium-filled balloons travel long distances and eventually rain back to earth in small pieces, which can survive intact in the ocean for as long as six months and can be eaten by sea turtles.

3. Avoid use of lights, fires, flash pictures, vehicles, loud noises, and even light-colored clothing on nesting beaches. Nesting females prefer dark, quiet beaches.

4. Hire local guides. They best know where and how to spot turtles and to prevent stressing the turtles while observing.

5. Do not feed turtles or any other wildlife. It can make them sick and more vulnerable to harm from people.

6. When boating, slow down when sea turtles are present to avoid colliding with them. Avoid anchoring in coral reefs and seagrass beds.

7. Eat local seafood caught with environmentally sensitive fishing gear, preferably troll or hook and line.

8. Maintain a respectful distance from all wildlife, on water or land.

9. When you vacation, reduce your carbon footprint, as climate change affects ocean wildlife.

10. Donate to or volunteer with local and regional conservation organizations (see a list in the Resources and Organizations section).

11. Spread the word about destinations that follow best practices; they need and appreciate your support.

Olive ridley in the morning. (Photo by Guillaume Feuillet)

A WORLDWIDE TRAVEL GUIDE TO SEA TURTLES

W E LIVE IN A WORLD of rapid and constant change, and perhaps nowhere is this more true than in conservation and work with wild animals and places. We made the information in this guidebook as accurate as possible at the time it went to press. However, budgets change, scientists and other personnel move on, and natural events such as storms or even earthquakes alter the physical environment. Governments change, economies rise and fall, and events around the globe affect sea turtle populations in far-flung areas. Given all that, before you travel to one of the destinations mentioned here, please confirm that it is still able to meet your needs.

The underlying themes of our book are that sea turtle encounters change lives and that ecotourism and "voluntourism" are key to saving sea turtles. But given remote locations, limited resources, and significant challenges, some projects simply cannot accommodate visitors at certain times. We appreciate your understanding and your support of sea turtles. Remember there are always many things you can do right at home to help.

A green sea turtle in the ocean near Hawai'i.
(Photo © Neil Ever Osborne; www.neileverosborne.com)

United States

🦑 California and the West Coast

W HILE NO SEA TURTLES nest on beaches of the US West Coast, most species do pass through or forage in its waters. Sharp-eyed kayakers may see green turtles in San Diego Bay or leatherbacks in Monterey Bay in the fall. Scientists from the National Oceanic and Atmospheric Administration's (NOAA) Southwest Fisheries Science Center have determined that waters off central California are a critical foraging area for one of the largest remaining Pacific leatherback nesting populations in Papua New Guinea. Loggerheads, which have been reported in the Pacific as far north as Alaska and as far south as Chile, are occasionally sighted off the coasts of Washington, Oregon, and California—primarily juveniles and subadults in California waters. Olive ridleys migrate from Pacific coastal breeding and nesting grounds out to pelagic foraging areas; ships crossing the Pacific have reported olive ridleys more than 2,400 miles from shore.

Leatherback Watch

Pacific leatherback sea turtles traverse the Pacific Ocean to forage on jellyfish off the West Coast of the United States. In 2012, NOAA's Fisheries Office of Protected Resources designated a 41,914-square-mile area off the coasts of Washington, Oregon, and California as critical habitat for leatherbacks. NOAA states that the greatest causes of decline and continuing primary threats to leatherbacks worldwide are long-term harvest and incidental capture in fishing gear. Incidental capture primarily occurs in gillnets but also in trawls, traps and pots, longlines, and dredges. Juveniles and adults are harvested in feeding grounds in the Pacific, while harvest of eggs and adults occurs on nesting beaches.

The Leatherback Watch Program, a project of the Sea Turtle Restoration Project (STRP), is a citizen science project working to record date, time, and GPS coordinates for sightings of leatherbacks in a database that can be used for education, research, and conservation purposes. The program launched in 2010 with one sighting in the Monterey Bay National Marine Sanctuary; 23 sightings were reported in 2011, beginning with one on June 29 off Point Sur; and 26 were recorded in 2012, with the majority seen in July. Any naturalist, whale watcher, fisher, or scientist can participate in the program by contacting the STRP. The database includes photos and video.

The Leatherback Watch Program database adds significantly to limited information available on habitat use and behavior of this critically endangered leatherback population. It has been used as an outreach tool and in advocacy aimed at providing additional protections to the sea turtles. Each year, the program hosts special expeditions to look for sea turtles offshore in San Francisco Bay. Trips are listed at seaturtles.org/events.

More information:
Sea Turtle Restoration Project: seaturtles.org/leatherbackwatch
Leatherback Watch: facebook.com/pages/Leatherback-Watch-Program/238320636189659

Sea Turtle Restoration Project

The Sea Turtle Restoration Project, based in Forest Knolls, north of San Francisco, "seeks to protect and restore endangered sea turtles and marine biodiversity worldwide in ways that incorporate the ecological needs of marine species and the economic needs of local communities, both of which share our common marine environment," according to the nonprofit's mission statement. STRP works to educate the public and policy makers and promote sustainable local, national, and international marine policies—resorting to litigation when necessary.

Biologist and activist Todd Steiner founded the organization in 1989 after learning that sea turtles he worked to protect in Central America were legally slaughtered after migrating into Mexican waters. STRP helped compel Mexico to end that then-legal harvest of sea turtles; it also helped enact use of turtle-saving gear in shrimping practices of 20 countries; helped create policy for the Leatherback Conservation Area on the West Coast, a 200,000-square-mile area closed to drift gillnet fishery in 2001; and sponsored legislation to designate the Pacific leatherback as the official marine reptile of California and October 15 as Pacific Leatherback Conservation Day.

STRP also has an office in Costa Rica and a sister organization in Papua New Guinea, and it is the largest project of Turtle Island Restoration Network, a 501(c)(3) organization. Turtle Island also sponsors projects on endangered salmon, shark conservation, and toxic mercury in seafood. It works to protect and restore marine species and their habitats and to inspire people around the world to become vocal marine species advocates.

STRP encourages involvement by volunteers and offers an advocacy and conservation policy internship at its California office. It conducts spotting trips for the Leatherback Watch Program, puts on events such as movie nights and beach cleanups at various California locations, and arranges other events around the world, including expeditions to help with research and conservation of sea turtles and other marine life. Find a schedule of coming events on the STRP website.

In 2002, STRP and a Texas organization, Helping Endangered Animals—Ridley Turtles (HEART), merged. HEART was founded by Carole Allen in Galveston in 1982, following her visits to the NOAA laboratory there (read more about the lab in the Captive Encounters section). Through STRP, Allen pushes for enforcement of regulations that require shrimp trawlers to have properly installed and functioning TEDs, seeks establishment of a turtle sanctuary in Texas Gulf waters to protect nesting ridleys, and campaigns for the US Fish and Wildlife Service to declare the upper Texas coast as critical habitat for Kemp's ridleys.

More information:
Sea Turtle Restoration Project: 800-859-7283, 415-663-8590,
    seaturtles.org

How to help:
Join the action alert list at seaturtles.org. Help fund STRP by shopping in the Sea Turtle Store online, adopting a turtle, or donating by visiting seaturtles.org and clicking on "Donate Now."

🐢 *Florida*

With 600-plus miles of beaches, Florida attracts more sea turtles than any other US state and accounts for some 90 percent of the nests in this country. Between 700 and 1,000 leatherbacks nest on Florida beaches each year, with a single female nesting an average of seven times during a season. Anywhere from 4,000 to 15,000 green sea turtles nest here each year as well. Florida is also the main nesting area in the United States for loggerheads, with as many as 70,000 nests in a single year. This state and a beach in Oman account for about 80 percent of all loggerhead nests in the world.

US sea turtle conservation efforts began here, and Florida continues to strive to be sea turtle–friendly. When you come to see and enjoy sea turtles, you help support existing protection and conservation efforts and show those in positions of authority that sea turtles are an important economic and cultural asset. Look for other, more specific ways you can help in the information about each area.

Archie Carr National Wildlife Refuge

This patchwork of protected federal, state, county, and private properties stretching 20 miles along the Atlantic coast of Florida near Sebastian represents one of the most significant sea turtle conservation and protection initiatives in the United States. It bears the name of a prominent figure in the world of sea turtle biology, Archie Carr, a former ecology professor at the University of Florida. In 1959, Carr founded the first sea turtle research and conservation organization, the Caribbean Conservation Corporation, now the Sea Turtle Conservancy.

Designation of the Archie Carr National Wildlife Refuge (NWR) counts as one of the state's key sea turtle conservation accomplishments, according to Blair Witherington, formerly with the Florida Fish and Wildlife Conservation Commission Research Institute. Its founding was based upon nesting data, so "the turtles themselves indicated where the refuge should be," he says. Not all identified nesting areas have been acquired, but the refuge, established in early 1990s, remains one of the most important loggerhead nesting sites in the Western Hemisphere, and more green sea turtles nest here than anywhere else in the United States. Leatherbacks nest inside the refuge as well. In 2012, the refuge recorded 18,958 loggerhead, 3,012 green, and 50 leatherback nests.

The Barrier Island Sanctuary Management and Education Center serves as the unofficial visitor center for the refuge, and the Sea Turtle Conservancy and US Fish and Wildlife Service offer guided sea turtle walks starting here Tuesday, Wednesday, and Friday nights in June and July from 9:00 p.m. to around midnight. The center takes reservations beginning May 1, and spots fill up within a few weeks. Groups are limited to 20 people, and a donation (currently $15) is required. Bring mosquito repellent and water, and be prepared to walk some distance on the beach and stay out as late as midnight. (Walks are therefore not recommended for very young children, the elderly, or people with disabilities.) The center holds monthly free events and offers occasional workshops and presentations on various aspects of sea turtle research and conservation, usually at no charge.

Visitors can volunteer for regularly scheduled daytime beach clean-ups, while those able to make a long-term commitment can train as volunteer turtle scouts, walking a section of beach at night while watching for nesting turtles.

More information:
Archie Carr NWR: 772-469-4275, fws.gov/archiecarr
Barrier Island Center: 8385 South Highway A1A, Melbourne Beach;
    321-723-3556, barrierislandcenter.com

How to help:
Support research, protection, and recovery programs by becoming a member of or donating to the Sea Turtle Conservancy. The organization also has hands-on volunteer opportunities in Costa Rica (see more in the Central America section).

Dry Tortugas National Park

The Dry Tortugas, a cluster of seven sandy coral islands 70 miles from Key West across open water, became a wildlife refuge in 1908 and a national park in 1992. These islands contain the largest green and logger-head nesting grounds in the Florida Keys, with some 15,000 hatchlings each summer. Kemp's ridley and hawksbill sea turtles also frequent the islands, and lucky visitors may spot sea turtles swimming in the clear, blue water. Park biologists have monitored nesting activity on all the islands since 1980. Nests are marked, recorded, and, 45 days later, checked for hatching. Researchers free any trapped hatchlings and count the number of eggs in each nest.

The Dry Tortugas served as strategic harbor for ships traveling between the Atlantic Ocean and Gulf of Mexico as early as 1513, and in 1846, the United States began constructing Fort Jefferson on Garden Key in hopes of controlling that maritime traffic. Work continued until 1889, but engineering challenges and military advances rendered the fort obsolete, and the hexagonal, three-tier brick behemoth remains unfinished.

Every day, weather permitting, the *Yankee Freedom* high-speed catamaran takes up to 120 tourists on a two-hour ride out to Garden Key. There, you have about four hours to tour the sprawling fort, snorkel, fish, bird-watch, and explore the beach. The price includes breakfast and lunch served on the boat. Those who want to stay overnight in the primitive campground can pack their gear on the boat and catch a return ride home after up to 14 nights. Grills, picnic tables, compost toilets, and posts for hanging food are available, but no water or other services. You can also bring kayaks along on the ferry to explore nearby Loggerhead and Bush Keys (Bush is closed February to September for nesting sooty terns, and Hospital and Long Keys are not open to the public).

More information:
Dry Tortugas National Park: 305-242-7700, nps.gov/drto

How to help:
   In the Keys, if you see lighting that may interfere with nesting or hatchlings or beach furniture left out overnight, contact Save-A-Turtle at 305-743-9629 or save-a-turtle.org. This nonprofit organization is dedicated to protecting sea turtles in the Keys and beyond; trained and permitted volunteers patrol local beaches during nesting season, and its monthly meetings at the Marathon Turtle Hospital are open to the public (read more about the Marathon Turtle Hospital in the Captive Encounters section).

Other things to do in the area:
   Eco-Discovery Center. Watch fish swim in a 2,400-gallon aquarium, explore a mockup of the underwater ocean laboratory Aquarius, watch a movie about the Keys, and browse exhibits about the marine ecosystem and its inhabitants—all free. The center is operated by the Florida Keys National Marine Sanctuary, NOAA, South Florida Water Management District, National Park Service, and National Wildlife Refuges and Eastern National. 305-809-4750, floridakeys.noaa.gov
   Key West Aquarium. Built in the 1930s as part of the Works Progress Administration program near the Key West Bight, the aquarium's walls are lined with tanks full of colorful marine life, with large shark, ray, and sea turtle tanks in the middle. Outside are two large pools, home to sea turtles too injured for release. There are also a touch tank, an alligator exhibit, shark feeding, and a jellyfish exhibit. Tickets are $15.05 for adults

and $7.53 for children ages 4 to 12 (discounts online). 888-544-5927, keywestaquarium.com

Palm Beach County

Palm Beach County has the highest number of leatherback nests and second-highest number of green and loggerhead nests in the country, with some 14,000 total nests on its 45 miles of beach each year. Three places in the county offer guided sea turtle encounters: Loggerhead Marinelife Center in Juno Beach, John D. MacArthur Beach State Park in North Palm Beach, and Gumbo Limbo Nature Center in Boca Raton.

The 325-acre John D. MacArthur Beach State Park surrounds Lake Worth Lagoon, a thriving estuarine system, and has 2 miles of beach. Arrive early in the day to kayak, snorkel, hike the trails, bird-watch, or just relax on the beach, but the main attraction, sea turtle nesting, occurs after dark. More than 1,000 loggerhead sea turtles nest on that beach from early May through late August every year, along with about 500 greens and 50 or more leatherbacks.

Sea turtle walks start with an orientation in the park's William T. Kirby Nature Center. Groups then file out of the theater to walk the boardwalk across the lagoon, finding footing by the light of the stars and a few small flashlights, then through the hammock and over the dunes. Here, everyone switches off the flashlights and waits quietly on the deck, crouched low and talking in whispers, until scouts on the beach find a female coming ashore.

Once the turtle digs a nest chamber and begins laying eggs, the group moves to the beach to watch, forming a semicircle around the dark, sandy body. Remember that the mother turtle enters an almost trancelike state, which allows observers to come fairly close without disturbing her. The nesting process takes about 45 minutes, but the length of the turtle walk will depend on how long it takes scouts to locate a nesting female.

The Marinelife Center has turtle walks Wednesday through Saturday evenings in June and July on adjacent beaches. In 2012, on the 9.8 miles from Juno Beach to Tequesta, those monitoring the beach counted 11,522 loggerhead, 1,361 green, and 287 leatherback nests. Scouts patrol the beach while people who have signed up to participate in a walk browse the exhibits on sea turtle biology, threats, and research with touch boxes, models, and skeletons. There are several indoor aquaria and outside

A loggerhead sea turtle swimming. (Photo by Bethany Resnick)

tanks with adult turtles undergoing rehabilitation at the center's turtle hospital. Once a nesting turtle is located, the group moves to the beach to watch. Walks are limited to 25 people and cost $17 with reservation and $20 for walk-ins (spots not guaranteed without a reservation). Children must be at least 8 years old to participate, and everyone needs to be able to walk perhaps as far as a half mile in the sand.

The Gumbo Limbo Nature Center opened in 1984 on 20 acres of barrier island with 5 miles of beach. Its mission is to increase public awareness of coastal and marine ecosystems. A boardwalk and trails traverse a lush hardwood hammock ecosystem where gumbo limbo, strangler fig, and cabbage palm trees grow. A 400-foot observation tower provides a bird's-eye view of the center, and the boardwalk leads to the city of Boca Raton's Red Reef Park. There are a butterfly garden, trails, and open pavilions covering tanks that represent four South Florida marine habitats. A sea turtle rehabilitation facility treats cold-stunned, sick, and injured animals. From late May to early July, the center offers sea turtle walks (with about 60 percent seeing a nesting turtle) Tuesday through Thursday in June, beginning at 9:00 p.m. It is one of only three facilities in Florida that has public hatchling releases, Monday through Thursday at 9:00 p.m. from late July through September. Both events cost $15 per person, require reservations, and sell out quickly.

More information:
John D. MacArthur Beach State Park: 561-624-6950, floridastateparks
   .org/macarthurbeach/default.cfm
Loggerhead Marinelife Center: 561-627-8280, marinelife.org
Gumbo Limbo Nature Center: 561-544-8605, gumbolimbo.org

How to help:
   Report lights visible on the beach to the Palm Beach County Department of Environmental Resources Management: 561-233-2400. Avoid using flashlights or building fires on the beach March through October. Become a member of the Loggerhead Marinelife Center or the Gumbo Limbo Nature Center.

Other things to do in the area:
   Key Biscayne National Park. The ocean covers 95 percent of this park, popular with boaters, fishers, snorkelers, and divers yet within sight of Miami. Camping is allowed on Boca Chita and Elliott Keys, accessible only by boat. You can drive to the Visitor Center at Convoy Point, where you will find exhibits, a theater, picnic tables, and a short trail. A concessionaire here offers boat tours or snorkeling and diving trips and rents kayaks, canoes, and paddleboats. Park: 305-230-7275, nps.gov/bisc; Concessionaire: 305-230-1100, biscayneunderwater.com

Museum of Discovery and Science. A variety of exhibits, from Florida's ecosystems, to the Everglades, river otters, hurricanes, space, and minerals, and an IMAX theater. 954-467-6637, mods.org

City Lights

The city of Fort Lauderdale has an ordinance that states "no artificial light shall illuminate any area of the incorporated beaches" in the city. The state of Florida classifies disturbing, destroying, causing to be destroyed, or otherwise interfering with sea turtles, their eggs, or nests as a third-degree felony.

Many businesses do their best to help the turtles. Lago Mar Resort, fronting 500 feet of wide, deep beach just south of Fort Lauderdale's main beaches, retrofitted its outdoor lighting, and during nesting season, staff bring in beach chairs at night to make it easier for turtles to nest. The hotel has been owned by a local family for more than 50 years, and the current manager says helping sea turtles is important to his guests.

Sea Turtle Oversight Protection (STOP), a nonprofit organization based in Fort Lauderdale, monitors the beaches throughout Broward County, patrolling public beaches at night and marking nests. The good news is that in 2012, STOP recorded 1,219 nests in Fort Lauderdale, Hollywood, Pompano Beach, and Hillsboro. The bad news is that, despite ordinances and good-faith efforts such as those of Lago Mar, the hatchlings from 38 percent of the recorded nests are disoriented due to lights, along with an unknown number of those from unmonitored nests.

Sebastian Inlet State Park

Part of the Archie Carr NWR, this state park has offered sea turtle walks for more than 30 years, and park services specialist Terry O'Toole has led them that entire time. Walks take place Friday through Wednesday nights in June and July and are limited to 20 people. Walks start at 9:00 p.m. with a presentation and Q&A while scouts out on the beach look for nesting turtles. Once the scouts find a turtle nesting, the group heads to the beach to observe. The entire process may take until midnight. If the scouts are not successful, sometimes O'Toole takes the group out to help look; he says walk participants see a nest 85 percent of the time. In 2012, some 1,100 loggerheads nested on the park's 3 miles of beach.

Sebastian Inlet State Park is home to the Fishing Museum and the McLarty Treasure Museum. Camping is available here and at Long Point Park. Many of the refuge sections have beach access or hiking trails, fishing, and bird-watching.

More information:
Sebastian Inlet State Park: 321-984-4852, floridastateparks.org/
    sebastianinlet/default.cfm

How to help:
To protect nesting turtles and prevent hatchling disorientation from lighting, report bright lights to 772-226-1249.

Other things to do in the area:
Environmental Learning Center (ELC), Vero Beach. November through April, the center offers pontoon excursions to Pelican Island, the Indian River, and the C54 canal (a good place to see manatees). Check the website for tour dates. The ELC also offers guided kayak trips to Wabasso and Pelican Island and two canoe trips per week from the ELC campus. Exhibits and trails are open year-round, and you can dial in to a cell phone tour of the trails, narrated by an animated local radio personality. Green and juvenile loggerhead sea turtles live in the lagoon year-round, so you may see them on kayak or canoe tours. A county lighting ordinance helps protect nesting turtles and prevent hatchling disorientation. 772-589-5050, discoverelc.org

Pelican Island National Wildlife Refuge. The first of the nation's wildlife refuges, Pelican Island was established by President Theodore Roosevelt on March 14, 1903, at the urging of local resident Paul Kroegel. Self-styled protector of the island's nesting white pelicans, who were being shot for feathers, sport, and supposed competition with fishers, Kroegel was appointed the first national game warden on April 1 and served until 1926. Visitors can take a tour, look out over Pelican Island from an observation tower, or hike trails through coastal jungle and mangroves. 772-581-5557, fws.gov/pelicanisland/

Capt Christy's "Casual Cruisin." Christy offers two- and three-hour pontoon boat tours to observe dolphins, manatees, birds, and whatever else she finds. She follows no set route but explores around the spoil islands, Pelican Island, and the lagoon, the most bioproductive estuary in the United States. Cruises leave from Sebastian Marina, and kayak tours put in from Pelican Island Refuge. 772-633-0987, http://www.captchristylenz.com/

Blowing Rocks Preserve. Loggerheads and some greens and leatherbacks nest on this Nature Conservancy preserve, which has a native plant demonstration garden and three hiking trails and boardwalks with interpretive signs, including a sea grape path to the Blowing Rocks, chunks of Anastasia limestone that create geysers from the waves. Swimming, snorkeling, and diving are allowed from the beach. The Hawley Education Center's exhibits include information on sea turtles. Open daily 9:00 a.m. to 4:30 p.m.; $2 fee for adults, and children 12 and younger free. 561-744-6668, nature.org/ourinitiatives/regions/northamerica/unitedstates/florida/placesweprotect/blowing-rocks-preserve.xml

St. George Island

Sea turtles nest on this 22-mile-long barrier island in the Florida Panhandle from May 1 to October 31, mostly loggerheads but also greens and leatherbacks. Volunteer organizations patrol 12 miles of beach on this island, 6 miles on nearby Alligator Point, and all beaches on Dog Island.

Nine miles of pristine beach in St. George Island State Park see 75 to 80 nests per year, nearly all of them loggerheads. Park staff patrol the beach daily May through October to mark nests and cover them with a protective screen. When nests start hatching, park staff and volunteers conduct an evaluation 72 hours after emergence, digging up and counting the number of hatched and unhatched eggs. The vast majority of hatchlings make it successfully out of the nest, says park manager Joshua Hudson, who calls them "the most adorable things in the world."

The park has picnic shelters on the beach, biking on the park road, and on the bay side, a full-facility campground, 2.5-mile nature trail, primitive campsites, and boat ramps for shallow-draft boats and kayaks. Kayakers often spot eagles and osprey in the tall trees on the back side of the island. Fish for flounder, redfish, pompano, and other catches in the surf or bay.

Outside the state park, beach monitoring has been coordinated since 1998 by Bruce Drye, first a volunteer, now part-time volunteer coordinator for the Apalachicola National Estuarine Research Reserve (ANERR). He relies on the assistance of resident volunteers and interns to walk sections of the beach first thing each morning, placing posts and signs around each nest and screening them from predators.

In 2012, the island's 12 miles of beach outside the park had 288 nests, with 45 of them laid in one week. Nesting activity and hatching both peak around July 4. Unfortunately, Drye says, 40 percent of hatchlings are lost, becoming disoriented due to artificial lights or becoming trapped in chairs, coolers, and other beach gear left out overnight. Franklin County has an ordinance requiring that house lights be turned off or shielded at night during nesting season, but enforcement is a challenge, and the rules do not apply to the island's small downtown area. He offers help with lights and even gives away some fixtures and LED lights. Red and amber LED lights are best, as these are the hardest for turtles to see. He also sells turtle-safe flashlights.

Drye holds sea turtle programs every Wednesday at the ANERR facility just across the bridge and says about 800 people a year attend. Island visitors can see nests marked on the beach, and anyone who happens upon Drye conducting an evaluation can watch. People can also see turtles in the water all summer long, he says, especially during nesting season, as females loiter while waiting to come in and nest.

More information:

Dr. Julian G. Bruce St. George Island State Park: 850-927-2111, floridastateparks.org/stgeorgeisland/default.cfm

St. George Island: 866-914-2068, saltyflorida.com

How to help:

Report signs of a turtle coming onto the beach, or crawl signs, to park staff; Bruce Drye, 850-927-2103; or the Florida Wildlife Commission, 888-404-3922. Avoid marked nests on the beach. Turn off outside lights and close blinds after dark. When renting a beach house, request one that is turtle-friendly—one with window coverings and outside lights that can be turned off (some automatic lights cannot be).

Other things to do in the area:

Apalachicola National Estuarine Research Reserve. This facility has exhibits on the natural area, aquariums, and programs. 850-670-7700, dep.state.fl.us/coastal/sites/apalachicola/

Apalachicola Maritime Museum. The museum has displays on the rich maritime history of the area and offers excursions on the *Starfish Enterprise*, a 36-foot power catamaran, to nearby uninhabited St. Vincent Island National Wildlife Refuge. 850-653-2500, ammfl.org

Journeys of St. George Island. This local outfitter offers kayak, sailboat, and catamaran rentals; guided kayak tours; guided boat tours including historical, river, bird, and sunset tours and dolphin encounters; and kids' adventures in summer. Kayaks are a great way to explore around St. George Island. 850-927-3259, sgislandjourneys.com

St. Joseph Peninsula

St. Joseph Peninsula and Cape San Blas are located off the Florida Panhandle and on a map look like a hitchhiker's thumb. They sit on two parcels of land: one is immediately south of the state park beach in the St. Joseph Bay Aquatic Preserve, managed by Gulf County; and the other is immediately south of that, owned by Eglin Air Force Base on the tip of the peninsula. Biologist Meg Lamont oversees the US Geological Survey (USGS) sea turtle program in this area. Her responsibilities include daily morning surveys May 1 through September 1 conducted by volunteers and paid interns, following protocols established by the Florida Fish and Wildlife Conservation Commission. Monitoring continues through November 1 to document hatching, and all nests are excavated to determine emergence success. From mid-May through mid-August, paid technicians conduct nightly tagging surveys in an effort to tag every turtle that nests within a study site that includes approximately 13 miles of beach.

Lamont welcomes volunteers for the morning surveys; anyone interested in riding along can contact her. She sometimes allows volunteers on night surveys, too, but because the work involves directly handling animals, she has to be more selective about who can participate.

Jessica McKenzie runs a USGS and University of Florida monitoring program in a residential area from Stump Hole, where the peninsula starts, to the boundary of St. Joseph Peninsula State Park, about 6 miles of beach. She accepts volunteers for morning patrols; a long-term commitment is preferred, but visitors can volunteer for just a day.

More information:
Meg Lamont: 352-209-4306, mmlamont@mindspring.com
Jessica McKenzie: 205-910-4717, jmbama@gmail.com

How to help:
Do not dig in the sand or push umbrella poles into the beach during nesting season. Use turtle-safe flashlights when on the beach after dark. In winter, volunteer to patrol for cold-stunned turtles or drive them to rehabilitation centers.

Other things to do in the area:
T. H. Stone Memorial St. Joseph Peninsula State Park. This park encompasses a sparkling white beach rated number one in the country in 2001 by Dr. Beach (a beach can be number one on his list only once). Turtles like it, too—nearly 200 nests were recorded here in 2012. The park includes nature trails, picnic area, campsites in some of the last remaining coastal sand pine scrub habitat, and eight cabins overlooking St. Joseph Bay. 850-227-1327, floridastateparks.org/stjoseph/

Gulf Islands National Seashore. Located in both Mississippi and Florida, this mostly underwater park contains white beaches made of fine quartz eroded from the Appalachian Mountains. Green, Kemp's ridley, and leatherback turtles nest here, but loggerheads are by far the most common. Nesting season runs May to September. The Mississippi section has a visitor center, boat launch, nature trails, campground, and boardwalk. In season, a ferry takes visitors to West Ship Island, and private boats can travel to any of the barrier islands. The Florida district's three sections include hiking trails, a bike loop, fishing, camping, beaches, boat launches, and ranger programs. Florida, 850-934-2600, nps.gov/guis; Mississippi, 228-875-9057

Florida's Nesting Beach Survey Program

On a designated set of beaches across Florida, scientists and managers collect data on sea turtle nests that help assess nesting trends, serving as a finger on the pulse of how well sea turtles are doing in Florida. Former program coordinator Blair Witherington, a senior biologist at the University of Florida Archie Carr Center for Sea Turtle Research, previously served as president of the International Sea Turtle Symposium and a member of the Loggerhead Sea Turtle Recovery Team. The department's other research projects include measuring the density and studying the behavior of pelagic turtles, or those living in the open Gulf and Atlantic. This research has made the case that sea turtles are tightly associated with the *Sargassum* community. Florida has achieved something of a balance between development and protection of beaches, Witherington believes, but that balance will shift as sea level rises.

"We face very tough decisions on when we're going to defend property against rising sea and when we're going to get smart and move back a bit," he says. "In those battles, I'm afraid sea turtles will suffer a bit. The real bugaboo with sea turtle conservation is that an individual state can't completely protect them by managing what happens on our beaches and in our waters, or even in federal waters, because they swim far and wide," he adds. "Many grow up in the eastern Atlantic where other countries set hundreds of thousands, if not millions, of hooks. The number of turtles taken by those fisheries is still thought to be very high, and a little bit out of our control as a nation. The US fleet is arguably the most highly regulated in the world, but it's hard to regulate what happens in other fisheries." While consumers can play a role, and some conservation organizations have tried to educate consumers to make wise choices when buying seafood, learning where it comes from can be very difficult.

Tour de Turtles

In 2008, the Sea Turtle Conservancy launched the Tour de Turtles Migration Marathon. This three-month annual event follows the migration of tagged turtles from nesting beaches to far-flung parts of the planet. It serves as an educational and public awareness tool and just some good, clean fun. Tagged turtles depart from nesting sites in Florida, and as they travel, their locations and distance appear on interactive maps on the Tour de Turtles website, tourdeturtles.org. While the animals may not know it, they compete to swim the farthest distance in the three months of the race. Through the Causes Challenge, the swimmers also raise awareness about threats to the survival of their species. Past tours have generated more than 30,000 visitors to the website, along with hundreds of new educators who sign up each year. Tour de Turtles offers a range of activities on the biology of sea turtles and gives teachers free access to educational materials, quizzes, and lesson plans.

There were 13 turtles competing in 2012, and in 261 days, winner Calypso Blue swam 7,124 miles out into the North Atlantic, while the second-place entrant, Karma, traveled 5,021 miles. Both were leatherbacks. Third place went to Lady Marmalade, a loggerhead, at 3,607 miles; a green sea turtle, Vida, took sixth at 982 miles; and Pinney, a hawksbill, swam 761 miles, placing tenth. Take a quick look at individual tracks for the turtles, and you will see that they do not go straight from Point A to Point B but spend a lot of time exploring, backtracking, and loitering in different areas. The ultimate goal remains to help turtles, and anyone can participate in that endeavor. Check the website regularly. When tour time comes around, choose your turtle, and may the best reptile win.

🏴 *Georgia*

Northern Georgia includes the southern end of the Appalachian Mountains and the Chattahoochee National Forest. Its southern half, more gentle landscape, becomes coastal woodland and swamp nearer the border with Florida. The state's short coastline is called the Golden Isles, a 150-mile-long collection that includes Jekyll, Cumberland, St. Simons, and Sea Islands.

Georgia Sea Turtle Center, Jekyll Island

Once owned by wealthy families including the Rockefellers, this island is now a popular vacation destination with three public beaches. The Georgia Sea Turtle Center (GSTC) on Jekyll Island has sea turtle rehabilitation, research, and education programs, including guided turtle walk programs held June 1 through July 31 (except July 4) at 8:30 p.m. and 9:30 p.m. Groups are limited to 25 people, reservations are required, and these walks fill up quickly.

The experience begins inside with a 30-minute presentation about the center and sea turtles; after that, participants follow the guide in their own vehicles to the beach. Flashlights and camera lights are not allowed for the safety of the turtles. Guides carry special, turtle-friendly lights and do their best to locate a nesting turtle for everyone to watch. Cost is $14 per person for the walks, or $20 with admission to the center included. Behind-the-scenes tours through food preparation, holding, treatment, and surgery areas take place daily at 3:00 p.m., circumstances permitting, and cost $22.

Sundays, Wednesdays, and Saturdays during nesting season, the center also offers nest walks on the beach. You will explore barrier island ecology with the help of a guide, then meet a turtle patrol intern or staff member at a nest site to conduct posthatch excavation. This occurs when a nest that has hatched naturally within the past five to seven days is dug up to record contents and determine hatching success rate. These nests may contain hatched eggs, unhatched eggs, dead hatchlings, and live hatchlings. Most live hatchlings should have left the nest on their own at this point, though, so there is no guarantee of seeing live turtles.

Participants will help record data on an official data collection form and may keep it as a souvenir. These groups are limited to 25 people as well. Nest walks take place anytime from 7:00 a.m. to 9:00 a.m., depending on high tides. Participants will receive a confirmation call several days in advance and need to meet their guide in the center parking lot 15 minutes prior to their walk time. Cost is $14, which does not include center admission.

On both turtle and nest walks, children under age 18 must be accompanied by an adult. Due to the nature of the turtle walks, children must be at least 4 years old. All proceeds support the work of the center, which includes a variety of research, a marine debris initiative, and rehabilitation of sick and injured turtles (read more about the center in the Captive Encounters section).

The center also offers two programs that provide a look into the lives of sea turtle biologists: the "Egg-sperience Dawn Patrol" and "Ride with Night Patrol." For the former, participants meet at 7:00 a.m. at Great Dunes Park to help prepare for the day's work and then accompany biologists on the beach for hands-on experience locating nests, checking for signs of depredation, and conducting nest excavations. "Ride with Night Patrol" guests participate in Jekyll Island's sea turtle monitoring project, starting from Great Dunes Park at dusk to patrol beaches with biologists in search of nesting loggerhead sea turtles. Both experiences offer the chance to ask the center's experienced biologists just about anything turtle-related. There is a maximum of four people for these tours; Dawn Patrol costs $50 per person (minimum age four), and Night Patrol costs $100 (minimum age six).

More information:
Georgia Sea Turtle Center: 912-635-4444 after May 1 for reservations, georgiaseaturtlecenter.org, klee@jekyllisland.com

How to help:
Join the GSTC citizen science program, become a member, or adopt a sea turtle.

Other things to do in the area:
Bicycle tours. More than 20 miles of bicycle trails explore the island's beach, maritime forest, and marsh landscapes. Bike rentals available.
University of Georgia 4-H Tidelands Nature Center. This center covers the coastal ecosystem with touch tanks, live animals, guided nature walks and kayak tours, and canoe and paddleboat rentals.
Other tours. Dolphin tours, fishing charters, and horseback riding are also available on the island.

East Coast Sea Turtle Nest Monitoring System

Every year from May to September, several thousand residents and enthusiasts collect data on sea turtle nesting along 710 miles of coastline in North Carolina, South Carolina, and Georgia. The resulting database represents a revolution in sea turtle conservation and management, according to Michael Coyne, founder of SeaTurtle.org, which developed the system in collaboration with the South Carolina and Georgia Departments of Natural Resources (DNR) and the North Carolina Wildlife Resources Commission.

Observers report real-time nesting data for four species of turtles into the system. This allows for more timely management decisions, according to DuBose Griffin, sea turtle coordinator for the South Carolina DNR. The data prove crucial in monitoring populations, creating effective regulations to protect turtles, and helping to maximize reproduction of these threatened and endangered animals. Leaders of nest protection efforts in one area can quickly see what is happening in other areas. The system also makes it possible for any interested individual to watch the nesting season progress.

The 2009 season served as a test for the system, and by August of that year, the database contained a total of 3,349 reported sea turtle nests. This included 2,133 in South Carolina, 945 in Georgia, and 257 in North Carolina (as well as 7 in Texas and 7 in a test location). The system now includes data from Angola, Cape Verde, Costa Rica, El Salvador, Greece, Mexico, Nicaragua, São Tomé and Principe, St. Maarten, Syria, US Virgin Islands, Alabama, Florida, and Texas. See it for yourself at seaturtle.org/nestdb/.

⛳ *Hawai'i*

Hawai'i Volcanoes National Park

At least 70 million years of volcanism, migration, and evolution in the Hawaiian Island–Emperor Seamount chain created bare land from the sea and then covered it in unique ecosystems. Hawai'i Volcanoes National Park contains two of the world's most active volcanoes, Kīlauea and Mauna Loa. The most massive mountain on earth, Mauna Loa covers an estimated 19,999 cubic miles. The current summit of Mauna Loa stands about 56,000 feet above the seafloor, more than 27,000 feet higher than Mount Everest. The park contains rainforest, desert, alpine, and coastal landscapes.

Hawksbill sea turtles, called *honu 'ea* or *'ea* in Hawai'i, live in the waters around these islands and are known to nest on remote beaches on the island of Hawai'i, one on Maui, and at an unknown number of locations on Moloka'i. Nesting season runs late May to December. Three of the beaches on the remote coast of Hawai'i are protected in the park: Halape, Apua Point, and Keauhou.

Volunteers are accepted year-round at the park for various duties. To volunteer for turtle crew, you must commit to at least 10 weeks, due to the training needed. Volunteering for the turtle crew is not for everyone because of the physical demands and lack of sleep. Turtle crew members work from the end of February through December and, during nesting season, camp on the beach, patrol for nests, tag turtles, record data, protect nests from predators, and excavate nests posthatching. Dorm-style housing and a meal stipend are provided.

Educational talks given by the park's interpretation division sometimes include information about sea turtles, and "After Dark in the Park" evening programs are occasionally scheduled that may discuss nesting. Check the Schedule of Events on the park's website.

More information:

Hawai'i Volcanoes National Park: 808-985-6000, nps.gov/havo

For information on seasonal volunteering, visit volunteer.gov/gov
   (search keyword "turtles"), or contact the Hawksbill Project:
   808-985-6090

How to help:

Do not camp or build fires on nesting beaches. Keep your campsite clean of food scraps to avoid attracting predators such as mongoose and feral cats, which may then feed on eggs or hatchlings. Report turtle sightings to park rangers: note the time, date, and location of your sighting.

Other things to do in the area:

Explore the national park. Drive 11-mile Crater Rim Drive, hike an abundance of trails, and depending on conditions, view active lava flows.

North Carolina

Mountainous and wooded to the west, North Carolina has 300 miles of Atlantic coastline on its eastern side, which attracts nesting sea turtles May through August. The North Carolina Sea Turtle Project, run by the North Carolina Wildlife Resources Commission's Division of Wildlife Management, monitors nesting and strandings along the entire coast. In 2012, the project documented 1,069 nests laid by loggerheads, 23 by greens, 5 by leatherbacks, and 2 by Kemp's ridleys. The patrols leave nests in place but mark them with stakes and flagging and, where predators are a problem, cover them with wire cages. They then check the marked nests regularly and, when hatching time approaches, may put barriers

Research Proves It:
People Love Sea Turtles

In December 2000, Regina Woodrom Rudrud, now a maritime and fisheries anthropologist specializing in sea turtle conservation biology at the University of Hawai'i Mānoa, took a job with the Oahu Sea Turtle Stranding Response Team. It is officially known as the Sea Turtle Stranding and Salvaging Group (SSG) of the Marine Turtle Research Program (MTRP) of the National Marine Fisheries Service (NMFS) Honolulu Laboratory.

For nearly a decade, she received almost daily telephone calls from Hawaiian residents and visitors to the islands, reporting sea turtles they believed were in distress. Often these people would spend an entire day in the blazing tropical sun to keep a sea turtle cool and safe from harm until she arrived. "The willingness of so many different people to spend their valuable time in the aid of the sea turtle is what prompted my dissertation research," Rudrud says.

She saw people rejoice, cry, and almost come to blows over stranded sea turtles, which led her to ponder the cultural value of sea turtles in Hawai'i. As she points out, we can tell what a person values by looking at how that person spends his or her time and money—and people come from all over the world and all walks of life to spend time and money for the chance to interact with sea turtles here.

Rudrud conducted a pilot project that included hundreds of on-the-spot interviews with residents and tourists during SSG turtle stranding cases. She says that although people could not explain why they love sea turtles, they do. She also handed out 515 questionnaires on the North Shore of Oahu, where adult turtles can be seen close to and on the shore feeding and resting. Those questionnaires revealed that 300 people came to the North Shore specifically to see these creatures, 377 would return just to do so, and 308 were personally affected in a positive way by the sight.

Gift stores here report that sea turtle–related merchandise sells better than just about anything else, sometimes as much as 20 times more. People wear sea turtles on their bodies—as tattoos, T-shirts, and jewelry—on their cars in the form of bumper stickers and emblems, on homes, and even as logos or advertising images for businesses. People just seem drawn to sea turtles somehow, in Hawai'i and around the world. ■

up to create a safe pathway to the water for hatchlings. About three days after hatching, project staff excavate nests and record data, including the number of eggs and hatching success.

A number of programs in the state use volunteers for daily patrols. These opportunities are most suited to permanent or seasonal residents. Find links to these programs on the sea turtle project's website, seaturtle .org/groups/ncwrc/links.html.

Cape Hatteras National Seashore

Located on islands known as the Outer Banks, Cape Hatteras National Seashore includes miles of beaches, windsurfing hotspots, and calmer waters on the back side of islands popular for kayaking and canoeing. There are three visitor centers: on Ocracoke to the south, Bodie Island on the north, and a visitor center and museum in the iconic Cape Hatteras lighthouse on Hatteras Island.

Five species of sea turtles have been seen at the National Seashore or its surrounding waters: loggerhead, green, leatherback, Kemp's ridley and, rarely, hawksbill. This is considered the northernmost range for nesting of loggerheads, which count for the majority of nests here, with a handful of greens and the occasional leatherback. Staff documented a Kemp's ridley nest, the first here, in 2011. In 2008, the park service began restricting nighttime off-road vehicle activity on the beach during nesting season, and new rules established in 2012 prohibit nighttime driving on the beach during nesting season for sea turtles and endangered piping plovers. Much controversy has surrounded these rules, with some opponents fearing they would discourage tourism. However, in 2012, officials not only documented a record 222 sea turtle nests on the National Seashore but the Dare County Visitors Bureau reported that the county collected more occupancy taxes than ever before, thanks to the highest gross occupancy on record during the season. More sea turtles, it turns out, equal more tourism. This underscores the importance of wildlife conservation and wildlife watching to local economies.

Nesting season at the National Seashore runs May to September. Nests are marked with posts and tape, and when it is time for a nest to hatch, a volunteer "nest sits" from dusk until midnight or later, ready to ensure that hatchlings make it safely to the water. Beach visitors can chat with these volunteers about why the area around the nest is closed, what type of turtle laid the eggs, or any other turtle-related subjects.

Volunteers can apply for seasonal opportunities at volunteer.gov (enter "North Carolina" in the state box and "National Park Service" in the agency box). Training is provided, and volunteers are asked to commit to a minimum of several weeks.

Park rangers present interpretive talks at the park's visitor centers, including programs on sea turtles and some especially for kids, and the Cape Hatteras Junior Ranger book has a section on sea turtles. In spring and summer, a park ranger provides updates on beach happenings, including nesting information. Rangers occasionally allow the public to view nest excavations and hatchling releases. Both events are unpredictable and depend on conditions, so call ahead for details.

Light pollution remains an issue for sea turtles at Cape Hatteras National Seashore. It can cause sea turtles to return to the sea without laying eggs and hatchlings to become disoriented. In dark areas of the park without artificial light pollution, the waters of the Atlantic reflect starlight and moonlight, making it brighter than the land and drawing hatchlings naturally to the water. In other areas, where hatchlings head toward artificial lights, they likely never reach the surf.

More information:
Cape Hatteras National Seashore: 252-473-2111, nps.gov/caha
To volunteer: volunteer.gov (search by state and type of activity)

How to help:
If you see a nesting turtle on the beach, a nest, or a stranded sea turtle, report it to park biologists at 252-216-6892.

Close blinds and turn off unnecessary outside lights on beach houses. If you own a beach home, point outdoor lights downward, not outward, and use less powerful bulbs and fully shielded outdoor oceanfront lighting.

Use flashlights on the beach only when necessary. Free permits are required for beach fires, which are prohibited between 10:00 p.m. and 6:00 a.m. and within 100 feet of a marked sea turtle nest. Build your beach fire according to your permit to minimize its impact on turtle hatchlings. Remove all equipment from the beach at night.

Other things to do in the area:

Explore the National Seashore. Visitors can camp, windsurf, surf, fish, kayak, and canoe. The Seashore is a Globally Important Bird Area and a major resting and feeding spot for migrating birds. It also contains three historic lighthouses: Ocracoke, Bodie Island, and Cape Hatteras; the latter two are open for climbing, with Cape Hatteras's 257 stairs equaling a 12-story climb.

Ocracoke Island. The park is home to wild ponies, most likely descended from survivors of a sixteenth- or seventeenth-century shipwreck. These Banker ponies, actually a physically unique type of horse, can be seen from a viewing area north of the village of Ocracoke.

Outer Banks. This area has many historical sites, including Fort Raleigh National Historic Site and the Wright Brothers National Memorial. Near the latter, Jockey's Ridge State Park has high dunes that attract hang gliders.

Hammocks Beach State Park

In May, June, and July, loggerheads nest in this state park on Bear Island, which is accessible only by private boat or ferry. Camp here during the season for one of the few opportunities to observe, on your own, a turtle making her nest or hatchlings digging their way out of one. Throughout the summer, rangers hold educational programs about sea turtles. Nesting records have been kept on the island since 1975, with nightly patrols to measure and tag nesting females conducted since the late 1970s. In 2012, beach patrols recorded 25 nests.

More information:
Hammocks Beach State Park: 910-326-4881, www.ncparks.gov/Visit/
    parks/habe/main.php or facebook.comHammocksBeach?ref=
    ts&fref=ts</

How to help:
Adopt a nest during the season at seaturtle.org.

Pea Island National Wildlife Refuge, Hatteras Island

Pea Island National Wildlife Refuge, established in 1937, includes about 13 miles of beach on the northern end of Hatteras Island. Staff and volunteers have monitored and protected sea turtle nests in the refuge since 1980 and recorded 30 of them in 2012. The Pea Island Visitor Center opens 9:00 a.m. to 4:00 p.m. daily year-round (the refuge closes at night) and includes a gift shop. No driving is allowed on the beach. There are two short wildlife trails, a bird blind, and fishing access to both the ocean and Pamlico Sound.

Due to erosion and high public use, most nests on Pea Island would drown or be trampled if left in place. Volunteers patrol the beach early mornings from May through September and relocate most nests to a safer area. When it is time for the eggs to hatch, these Turtle Watch volunteers hold vigil, sitting with nests until hatchlings emerge and ensuring they make it safely into the ocean. Loggerheads lay most of the nests here, but occasionally a green sea turtle shows up.

To help with the sea turtle program, sign up as a general volunteer and attend training, held in May, for either turtle patrol (ATV training required) or nest watch. Then make yourself available on the volunteer schedule. Contact the volunteer coordinator, tracey_rock@fws.gov, or call 252-473-1132, ext. 227.

More information:
Visitor Center: 252-987-2394, fws.gov/peaisland/

How to help:
If you see crawl tracks or a sea turtle, report it to the Visitor Center. Join the Coastal Wildlife Refuge Society, which supports eastern North Carolina's Wildlife Refuges: 252-473-1131, ext. 230, coastalwildliferefuge.com.

🦃 *South Carolina*

The foothills of the Blue Ridge Mountains extend into South Carolina's northwestern corner, and its coast may be best known for icons such as Myrtle Beach on the northern end and Hilton Head Island on the south. The South Carolina Department of Natural Resources (SCDNR) Marine Turtle Conservation Program manages and protects sea turtles in the state. The program locates and protects sea turtle nests, documents strandings, monitors nearshore waters for leatherbacks, and works with the South Carolina Aquarium to rehabilitate live stranded turtles (read more about the program in the Captive Encounters section). The SCDNR began monitoring nesting in the late 1970s. Nesting surveys and nest protection are done by volunteers, researchers, and biologists from various agencies, including SCDNR, the US Fish and Wildlife Service, South Carolina Department of Parks and Recreation, and Coastal Carolina University. Between 1980 and 2007, these efforts affected more than 4.6 million loggerhead hatchlings. Some 186 miles of South Carolina beach are suitable for nesting, and loggerhead, green, leatherback, and even a few Kemp's ridley nests have been documented on them. Loggerheads outnumber the rest by far, with about 4,600 nests recorded in 2012; there were 7 green nests and 1 leatherback nest.

More information:
Marine Turtle Conservation Program: dnr.sc.gov/seaturtle/
Follow nesting during the season in real time: seaturtle.org/
    nestdb/?view=2
Follow strandings in real time: seaturtle.org/strand
Report nesting or stranded sea turtles: 800-922-5431

How to help:
South Carolina residents can order special endangered species license
    plates, with the fee supporting conservation and protection of the
    state's natural resources: dnr.sc.gov/admin/endangeredplate.html.

Cape Romain National Wildlife Refuge

Five-mile-long Cape Island, between the Santee Delta and Bulls Bay along the north-central South Carolina coast, is home to an average of 1,000 nests per year. For purposes of conservation and protection, the turtles nesting here are considered a northern subpopulation of the larger southeastern loggerhead population. This northern subpopulation, or nesting aggregation, includes loggerheads nesting from North Carolina south to around Cape Canaveral, Florida. These turtles are genetically distinct from all other nesting loggerheads in the southeastern United States.

Since 1980, a nest monitoring and management project at the refuge has transplanted nests into predator-proof hatcheries or caged nests in place to protect them, as well as kept an inventory of nests and conditions. The 2012 nesting season broke records with an official nest count of 1,671 from May to August: 1,130 of them on Cape Island, 350 on Lighthouse Island, 157 on Bulls Island, and 26 on Raccoon Key. Volunteers spent more than 5,000 hours helping to protect these nests.

More information:
Cape Romain National Wildlife Refuge: fws.gov/caperomain/
   turtleproject.html
To volunteer, contact the NWR: 843-928-3264; patricia_lynch@fws
   .gov; or go to fws.gov/caperomain/volunteers.html and click on
   "volunteer application" at the bottom of the page

How to help:
Adopt a nest at Cape Romain at seaturtle.org/nestdb/adopt/.

Edisto Island

Loggerheads nest on Edisto Island from April through October. At Edisto Beach State Park, which recorded 169 nests in 2012, turtle walks are held on Tuesday and Thursday nights in June at 9:00 p.m. These begin with a presentation about sea turtle biology, conservation, and challenges to their survival, followed by a walk of approximately 3 miles. The park also has hiking and biking trails, an environmental education center, cabins, and campsites.

Botany Bay Plantation Wildlife Management Area, 3,363 acres in the northeastern corner of the island just north of the Edisto River, is one of the largest remaining relatively natural wetland ecosystems on the Atlantic coast. The Wildlife Management Area (WMA) and Botany Bay Island, which is under conservation easement with The Nature Conservancy, provide important habitat for a variety of coastal wildlife, including nesting loggerheads. The WMA is open to the public daily (except Tuesdays) and offers hiking, biking, kayaking and canoeing, fishing, and driving tours. The staff offer turtle programs in season, and visitors can call or check the kiosk at the main gate off Botany Bay Road for scheduled programs.

More information:

Edisto Island State Park: 843-869-2156 (for turtle walks, call the interpretive center, 843-869-4430), southcarolinaparks.com/edistobeach/introduction.aspx (click on "Programs & Events")

Wildlife Management Area: 843-869-2713, https://www.dnr.sc.gov/mlands/managedland?p_id=57

To volunteer: call Bess Kellett at 843-442-8140

How to help:

If you encounter a sea turtle or hatchlings, do not approach or disturb them. If you find a dead, sick, or injured sea turtle, call the South Carolina Department of Natural Resources 24-hour hotline: 800-922-5431.

Other things to do in the area:

Edisto Island. About 45 miles south of Charleston, you can also enjoy deep-sea and surf fishing and sailing.

Sea Turtle Friend

Edwin Byrd Drane, known as Ed to his friends, deserves much of the credit for the natural character of South Carolina's Hilton Head Island. Thanks to Ed's work with the Savannah Coastal Wildlife Refuge, US wildlife refuges now sport signs, visitor displays, shelters, and parking areas that make them more visitor-friendly.

Ed's relationship with sea turtles began in 1985 when he became a member of the Hilton Head Turtle Watch, patrolling beaches for loggerhead nests and hatchlings. He later became involved in the International Sea Turtle Society, traveling all over the world for the cause and serving

A Kemp's ridley sea turtle at Padre Island National Seashore.
(National Park Service, Padre Island National Seashore)

as the organization's treasurer for 19 years. Ed died in 2009 and is buried in Bonaventure Cemetery in Savannah, but his spirit walks a sandy beach, keeping a sharp eye for turtle tracks.

🏴 *Texas*

The Texas coast covers nearly 400 miles, forming the western boundary of the large and incredibly biodiverse Gulf of Mexico. The warm, shallow Gulf, bays, estuaries, and marshes provide habitat for a wide range of creatures, including sea turtles. In recent years, nests from five sea turtle species have been documented on the Texas coast. The overall numbers are small, but more Kemp's ridleys nest here more often than anywhere else in the United States. In 2012, scientists documented 209 Kemp's nests, 5 loggerhead nests, and 8 green nests.

Padre Island National Seashore

As the summer sun appears over a watery horizon, Padre Island National Seashore staff lug a grocery store cooler to the edge of the Gulf of Mexico. Gloved hands scoop out the palm-sized Kemp's ridley sea turtle hatchlings inside and carefully place them on the beach a few yards from the surf. Rows of breakers hit the shallow shore with a hypnotic pounding, punctuated by the rising breeze and cry of seabirds. Long strips of cloth fluttering atop tall poles discourage those birds from coming close as the vulnerable hatchlings begin to scurry over sand and seaweed toward the water. At first, each wave sweeps the hatchlings back up the shore. But the turtles soldier on, front flippers churning like tiny propellers when they finally catch a wave that carries them out to sea. Some 30 minutes later, the last one disappears into the Gulf.

People come from far and wide to attend these public releases, held at dawn between June and August. Projected release dates are posted on the National Seashore's turtle hotline. Visitors from out of town are encouraged to plan on several days in the area and to call before leaving home and again the night before a release to confirm. The baby turtles, which generally hatch during the night, must be released before dawn if they grow too active, which could burn up energy they need to swim for several days to reach floating masses of *Sargassum* that provide cover from predators and plenty to eat until the turtles grow large enough to navigate the open sea. Late release of active hatchlings could actually cost them their lives.

Those who attend a hatchling release become part of one of the most intense, long-running, and successful sea turtle restoration projects in

Returning to the Gulf of Mexico. *(National Park Service, Padre Island National Seashore)*

the world. The public is a significant part of the turtles' recovery at the National Seashore, the most important Kemp's ridley nesting area in the United States. Tours and hatchling releases provide a good opportunity to educate people about threats to sea turtle survival and how simple changes in our behavior can help protect them.

In addition, members of the public locate about half of the nests documented in Texas. Unlike other sea turtle species, ridleys usually come ashore to nest during the day, when the ever-present sea breeze can blow away the nesting mother's tell-tale tracks in the sand. Small and light, ridleys leave only faint tracks on the beach in the best of conditions and take just about 45 minutes to crawl onto the sand, bury their eggs, and return to the water. While park staff and trained volunteers monitor 80 miles of Texas beach from March through July, there is simply too much beach for them to find all the nests.

Volunteers must attend training sessions, held in February and March at the National Seashore, and commit to at least one month of service (although some work the entire season). They then patrol designated areas in five-hour shifts, morning or afternoon. Cynthia Rubio, biologist and volunteer coordinator for the sea turtle program, says, "Finding a nesting turtle is an experience of a lifetime."

In the winter, volunteers are needed to help with strandings that occur when the temperature drops rapidly. Known as cold-stunning, this can cause turtles to become lethargic, and the animals need to be kept in a warm place until they recover and outdoor temperatures increase. Training sessions are held in the fall and early winter.

More information:
Padre Island National Seashore: 361-949-8068, nps.gov/pais
Public release hotline: 361-949-7163

How to help:
Volunteer for nest patrol or cold-stun events: 361-949-8173, ext. 228.

Watch for tracks or nesting turtles. If you see one, do not approach until the mother turtle begins laying her eggs. If she has a metal flipper tag, note the number. Once she has finished, mark the nest with beach material (do not push anything into the sand, as it might damage the eggs), and report the nest to 1-866-TURTLE-5. This number can be used to report a nest anywhere in Texas.

Pick up trash on the beach, and drive slowly. Do not fish in areas where a number of turtles are visible.

Other things to do in the area:
Padre Island National Seashore. In addition to the Ridley project, this park, occupying the longest undeveloped barrier island in the world at 60 undisturbed miles, offers plenty of other diversions. Between mile posts 0 and 5, beach maintenance makes it possible to drive cars and RVs; beyond marker 5, four-wheel drive is necessary. Wide beaches, gentle surf, tall dunes, and an ever-present sea breeze make it worth the effort, as does the solitude. Those who venture down the island enjoy starry skies, great fishing and beach combing, and finds such as the tracks of coyotes and the occasional sea turtle.

Just inside the park, the Malaquite Pavilion Visitor Center includes exhibits and touch displays, a bathhouse, park store, water fountains, and covered picnic tables. Malaquite Beach campsites have 24-hour access to showers and toilets in the pavilion. Primitive camping is allowed anywhere along the rest of the island (permits required, available at the visitor center). The Bird Island Basin section, on the Laguna Madre side of the island, has a designated windsurfing area and is popular for kayaking and fishing.

Mustang Island State Park. This park, south of Corpus Christi Bay across the intracoastal waterway, offers a sheltered stretch of beach, fishing jetty, camping and RV area, and a bathhouse with showers.

Texas State Aquarium. The aquarium showcases more than 300 species, mostly from the waters of the Gulf of Mexico, including exhibits of offshore platforms and the Flower Garden Banks National Marine Sanctuary, 100 miles off the Texas coast; jellyfish tanks; sea otters; dolphin shows; rescued sea turtles (read more in the Captive Encounters section); and the Hawn Wild Flight Theater (361-881-1200, texasstateaquarium .org).

South Padre Island

In 1977, Ila Loetscher founded a small nonprofit center on South Padre Island to treat injured turtles. Loetscher became known as the Turtle Lady for her work with these animals. But she garnered fame long before she saw her first Kemp's ridley, when she became, at 24, the first woman in Iowa to hold a pilot's license and soon after helped Amelia Earhart found the 99s, a group of women pilots. The organization has

Egg-Sniffing Dog

The nests of Kemp's ridley turtles can be nearly impossible to find in the deep, windblown sand of North Padre Island. Donna Shaver at Padre Island National Seashore trained two cairn terriers to sniff out turtle eggs. In the summer of 2008, one of them, Ridley, proved his worth. After beach patrollers spotted the tracks of a turtle, staff and volunteers searched for her nest for five hours. Finally, they called in Ridley, who immediately found the nest, making it possible for the team to take the eggs to safety in the turtle lab. Shaver will continue to use her dogs' talented noses and may train other dogs as searchers.

The Kemp's Ridley Restoration Project

LONG before human feet touched the sandy shores of the western Gulf of Mexico, tens of thousands of female sea turtles visited every summer to lay their eggs. Hatchlings emerged weeks later and scurried into the sea. After 10 or 15 years, many returned to make their own nests. For millennia, green, loggerhead, leatherback, and Kemp's ridley sea turtles continued making this shore part of their life cycle. But as the coast became the modern states of Texas and Tamaulipas, life grew difficult for the turtles. They drowned in fishing nets or on hooks. People ate adult turtles and their eggs. Development along Texas and Mexican beaches turned back nesting females. By the latter half of the twentieth century, all four of these species were endangered, and by the 1970s, not a single sea turtle nested on Texas shores. Only a few hundred Kemp's ridleys, once the most common Gulf species and now the most critically endangered, nested at all, solely on a remote beach in Mexico.

Then a dedicated cadre of scientists, government officials, businesses, and citizens sprang into action. They formed the multiagency, binational Kemp's Ridley Sea Turtle Restoration and Enhancement Project and began the long process of reestablishing nesting on Padre Island. From 1978 to 1988, scientists collected eggs in Mexico, incubated them in sand from North Padre Island, and released the baby ridleys on the island. The project marked released turtles with a living tag, a plug of lighter-colored undershell inserted into the upper shell, in a location on the turtle that indicated the year of release. Starting in 1986, with the possibility that some of those first turtles released had reached maturity, Padre Island National Seashore staff and volunteers began patrolling the beaches for signs of returnees. They occasionally found a nesting turtle but none that bore one of these living tags.

Then in 1996, Donna Shaver, chief of the park's division of sea turtle science and recovery, responded to a report of a nesting ridley and at last found what she had been looking for. "I brushed the sand off her carapace and saw the living tag," Shaver says. "I looked three times to be sure. I was ecstatic, after a decade of patrols not finding anything, to finally see the first one. To know this was one I had hatched and she had come back. To me it symbolized real hope for the future, the real possibility that all we worked for all those years would come to fruition." Until that day, scientists had only hope that nesting could be reestablished in Texas; now they had confirmation. More turtles returned each year, and, in 2012, some 106 Kemp's ridleys nested on North Padre, with more than 11,000 hatchlings released at the park.

Incubating eggs in the lab and shepherding the hatchlings safely to the water, as many sea turtle projects do, improves the hatchlings' rather dismal survival odds. For Kemp's ridleys, protecting nesting beaches in Texas and Mexico and reducing the take from commercial and recreational fishing through information campaigns and new devices have contributed to an encouraging rise in nests. Worldwide, the number of Kemp's ridley nests in a single year has approached 20,000.

But the species is still a long way from changing its endangered status. Drowning in shrimp nets remains a main cause of mortality, while harvesting of eggs, slaughter for food, and incidental capture by fishing operations continue. Propeller strikes, turtle entanglement in and ingestion of marine debris, and dredging are also major threats, Shaver says. The 2010 Deepwater Horizon disaster spilled more than 200 million gallons of oil into the Gulf of Mexico. After nesting, tagged female Kemp's ridleys have been tracked traveling into the area affected by the spill. Juveniles and adults forage there. More than 425 dead sea turtles were reported in the spill zone, and more have been killed when oiled Sargassum was burned. ∎

since grown to include not just 99 women pilots but thousands of them worldwide. After moving to South Padre Island, Loetscher began caring for sick and injured sea turtles in her home, then bringing ridley eggs from Rancho Nuevo to the island in the 1960s.

Today, Loetscher is gone, but Sea Turtle Inc. continues to patrol South Padre beaches for nests, maintain a protected area for incubating nests, and release hatchlings. During the summer, the public can observe hatchling releases, which peak around the Fourth of July. The facility also treats sick and injured turtles (for more information, see the Captive Encounters section).

A tiny gift shop at Sea Turtle Inc. sells beads made from recycled glass bottles in Trinidad, site of some of the major nesting beaches for leatherbacks. The beads provide alternative income for local people historically dependent on poaching the sea turtle's eggs, and their manufacture helps

Making tracks. (National Park Service, Padre Island National Seashore)

keep those beaches clear of glass debris. Sea Turtle Inc. provided the startup costs and training for this small industry. Visitors to the South Padre facility who purchase the beads therefore contribute directly to the economy of communities in Trinidad near nesting beaches, indirectly helping ensure survival of this ancient species.

The shop also sells purses hand-crocheted from discarded plastic bags in Gandoca, Costa Rica. Each messenger-size bag is made up of about 80 individual plastic bags. Women in the village are paid for each purse, with the funds benefiting their village and its leatherback conservation project. Coconut shell jewelry made at the nesting beach in Tamaulipas,

Mexico, and ceramics made near the beach (also sold at Brownsville's Gladys Porter Zoo) also help fund ongoing protection of nesting beaches and turtles.

More information:
Sea Turtle Inc.: 956-761-4511 (hatchling hotline, 956-433-5735), seaturtleinc.org

How to help:
Adopt a turtle from Sea Turtle Inc. or purchase some of its merchandise. Report nesting sea turtles or suspected nests to 1-866-TURTLE-5.

Other things to do in the area:
South Padre Island. This area attracts surfers, fishers, scuba divers, and beach lovers of every kind. Accommodations range from upscale hotels to beach condos and houses, on the beach side and on Laguna Madre Bay, a favorite place for those who like to fish, sail, and windsurf.

South Padre Surf Company. The company offers surfing lessons year-round, including one-day and week-long summer camps and holiday camps, at Isla Blanca Beach Park. Co-owner Gene Gore claims the park has the best surf in the Gulf of Mexico and says he has a 100 percent success rate in getting students to surf on their own by the end of class.

Schlitterbahn Beach Waterpark. One of a family of waterparks noted for innovation, Schlitterbahn includes a surf ride as well as dozens of others, along with an indoor water park and hotel.

South Padre Island Birding and Nature Center. One of nine World Birding Center sites, which has 4,800 feet of boardwalk and seven bird blinds in the Laguna Madre wetlands.

Colley's Fins to Feathers Dolphin and Birding Tours. Guided tours on a quiet boat with six or fewer people to see resident dolphins and a variety of sea- and shorebirds. Information at sopadre.com.

Tip: Pick Up Plastic

Pick up plastic on beaches and waterways, which carry it to the ocean. Many sea turtles eat jellyfish and eat floating plastic by mistake. Thousands of turtles die when this plastic clogs their digestive systems. ■

A young green sea turtle in the ocean. (Photo by Bethany Resnick)

Caribbean Islands

A STRING of islands arcing from Cuba, just 90 miles south of Florida, to the northern coast of South America rings clear, blue waters known as the Caribbean Sea. These islands include the Cayman Islands, Jamaica, Turks and Caicos, Puerto Rico, the British and US Virgin Islands, Dominican Republic, Haiti, Anguilla, Antigua and Barbuda, Aruba, Barbados, Bonaire, Grenada, Curaçao, Dominica, Guadeloupe, Martinique, Montserrat, Saba, St. Barthélemy, St. Eustatius, St. Kitts and Nevis, St. Lucia, St. Maarten, St. Martin, St. Vincent and the Grenadines, and Trinidad and Tobago. In all, this sea contains more than 7,000 islands, islets, reefs, and cays. Collectively they are known as the Greater Antilles—which includes Cuba, Haiti/Dominican Republic, Puerto Rico, and Jamaica and represents more than 90 percent of the total landmass—and the Lesser Antilles. Some are flat and primarily of coral reef origin, while others have a volcanic history and the rugged mountains to prove it.

The Caribbean Sea covers more than a million square miles, bordered by the North and South Atlantic Oceans to the north and east, South America to the south, and Central America, Mexico, and the Gulf of Mexico to the west and north. Its name comes from the Caribe, an ethnic group living here when Europeans arrived.

Those early Europeans documented vast populations of sea turtles in the Caribbean, flotillas of turtles so dense that they hindered ship movement and made it impossible to catch fish with nets. Sailors talked of so many turtles it looked as if a person could walk across the water on them. These were some of the largest breeding populations in the world, but most have disappeared. When the Cayman Islands were colonized in the 1600s, for example, they likely contained the largest nesting population of green sea turtles in the greater Caribbean basin. Adult turtles and eggs proved to be too-easily exploited resources, and by the early 1800s, turtle fishers could no longer catch turtles in the Cayman area at all.

Today, the main threats to Caribbean sea turtles include accidental capture in fishing gear, degradation of coral reef and seagrass habitat,

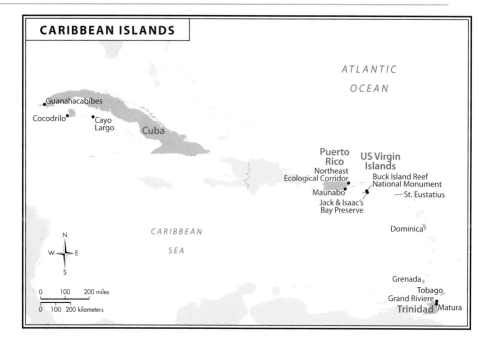

pollution, marine debris, and development. In addition, a regulated but largely unmanaged harvest of breeding-age adults continues in some countries. For small, remnant populations, the take of only a few nesting females each year can have an enormous effect. Leatherback, loggerhead, green, olive ridley, Kemp's ridley, and hawksbill sea turtles all spend time in some part of the Caribbean during at least some stage of their lives.

🐢 *Cayman Islands Sea Turtle Farming*

A sea turtle farm has operated in the Cayman Islands since the 1970s, raising green sea turtles for meat and products and releasing some hatchlings and yearlings in an attempt to boost the local wild population. The Cayman Turtle Farm has been the subject of much controversy, which you can read about in the Captive Encounters section.

Archie Carr, the Father of Sea Turtle Conservation

Biographer Frederick Rowe Davis called biologist Archie Carr "the man who saved sea turtles," and aptly so. Starting in the 1950s, Carr championed sea turtles, and his work created a conservation ethic and approach that underlie almost every effort currently under way. A herpetologist, Carr contributed greatly to the basic knowledge of sea turtle biology and natural history; he published more than 100 scientific papers, many on the ecology and migrations of sea turtles; and he published many popular and award-winning nature books as well as biology books, including *The Reptiles, The Land and Wildlife of Africa, The Everglades, Sea Turtles: So Excellent a Fishe, The Windward Road, High Jungles and Low, Ulendo: Travels of a Naturalist in and out of Africa,* and *A Naturalist in Florida: A Celebration of Eden. The Windward Road* inspired the founding of the Caribbean Conservation Corporation, now the Sea Turtle Conservancy (STC), in 1959. STC has supported hundreds of research projects on the biology and conservation of sea turtles, advocates for sea turtle conservation and protection, and monitors and protects a number of high-density nesting beaches.

Born June 16, 1909, in Mobile, Alabama, Carr grew up with a love of nature. His father was a Presbyterian minister; and his mother, a piano teacher. He received a PhD in zoology in 1937 from the University of Florida and taught and mentored students there for more than 50 years. In the 1950s, he took a four-year leave from the university to teach biology in Honduras and conducted research for six months in Africa, an experience that had a profound effect on his thinking. He spent two years teaching in Costa Rica in the 1960s. He and his wife, Marjorie Harris Carr, a biologist, had five children, all of whom became involved with conservation.

Carr proved instrumental in the formation of Tortuguero National Park in Costa Rica, the site of one of the longest-lasting and most intensive studies of an animal population ever. Tens of thousands of adult female green turtles have been tagged at the research station there, leading to dozens of research papers. Carr also served 20 years as chairman of the Marine Turtle Specialist Group of IUCN's Survival Service Commission.

Carr died at home on Wewa Pond near the town of Micanopy, Florida, on May 21, 1987. After his death, establishment of the Archie Carr National Wildlife Refuge in Florida protected the most significant area for loggerhead sea turtle nesting in the Western Hemisphere and the most significant green turtle nesting area in North America (read more about the refuge in the section on Florida). ■

✦ *Cuba*

This island, the largest in the Greater Antilles, sits at the confluence of the Gulf of Mexico, Atlantic Ocean, and Caribbean Sea. Cuba is actually an archipelago of several thousand islands and cays, all dwarfed by the 776-mile-long main island. Dubbed an "accidental Eden" by a PBS documentary, the country has largely pristine coasts and marine resources thanks to its low population density, progressive environmental legislation passed in the 1990s, and isolation due to a US government embargo in place since the 1960s. While government policy makes it difficult for US citizens to travel to Cuba, Canadians, Australians, South Americans, and Europeans travel there frequently.

Cayo Largo

This island lies south of the mainland of Cuba and east of the Isle of Youth, with more than 12 miles of white sand beach. Cayo Largo ranks as Cuba's main nesting site, with roughly 2,500 green and loggerhead nests annually. Eggs are collected from nests on some beaches where they are considered vulnerable and brought into a "turtle farm" to incubate; then the hatchlings are released on the beach. Visitors can visit the farm or participate in releases for a small fee.

There are a number of all-inclusive resort hotels, and tourists are allowed on the beach during nesting season; future plans call for organized turtle walks. Occasionally tourists are invited to witness a nesting turtle, but visitors should not go onto the beach at night without a guide. There are flights to the island from Havana and Varadero as well as charter flights directly from Canada, Europe, Mexico, and Grand Cayman. Two-day package excursions are available through a Cuban tour agency. Be forewarned: nude sunbathing is allowed on Cayo Largo.

More information:
Buro de Turismo: 045-24-8214
Cayo Largo: cayolargo.net/index.html

Cocodrilo Sea Turtle Festival

Cuba's 1,864 miles of coastline attract green, loggerhead, and hawksbill turtles. Two villages, Cocodrilo on the Isle of Youth off the southern coast and Nuevitas on the north-central coast, had since the 1960s harvested more than 500 hawksbills a year for meat and shell products. Under pressure from the international conservation community, the Cuban government placed a moratorium on this harvest in 2008. This led to an increase in the hawksbill populations but left fishers in isolated Cocodrilo without a livelihood.

The Ocean Foundation turned to Grupo Tortuguero, a community activism group in Mexico's Baja California peninsula, to discuss ways to help. Fishers in Baja California, conservationists, and biologists had formed Grupo Tortuguero to help develop alternatives to turtle fishing, such as ecotourism, research, and conservation (read more in the section on Mexico). At a Cuba-US-Mexico gathering on the Isle of Youth in 2009, participants decided to engage in outreach to the community to help fishers, women, and children understand the ecological and financial benefits of protecting turtles. They staged a sea turtle festival in Cocodrilo in November 2011, with educational workshops, a forum for local fishers, and music and poetry by local artists about marine conservation. A second festival, held in May 2012, sparked efforts to offer ecotourism in the area, such as tours of the Punta Frances reef and guided visits to El Guanal, a loggerhead turtle nesting beach. The Cuban Center for Fisheries Research, led by Felix Moncada, has conducted nest-monitoring research at El Guanal for more than three decades. Organizers plan to make the turtle festival an annual event each summer.

More information:

There is not as of yet (2013) a website for the area or festival.

How to help:

Support future festivals at Cocodrilo by donating to the Ocean Foundation's Cuba Marine Research and Conservation Program: oceanfdn .org/ocean-conservation-projects/listings/cuba-marine-research-andcon servation. If you visit Cuba and are on the Isle of Youth in the summer, attend the Sea Turtle Festival or pay a visit to Cocodrilo and the Lanier Swamp anytime (tourist permit required).

Guanahacabibes Sea Turtle Project

The 55-mile-long and 18-mile-wide Guanahacabibes Peninsula covers the westernmost tip of Cuba, on a route that migrating sea turtles take between Mexico and Florida. A UN Biosphere Preserve created in 1987 takes in the entire peninsula, much of which is also a national park. Green sea turtles nest here, and the University of Havana's Center for Marine Research has monitored this population during nesting season, May to September, for more than 15 years. Students from the university work two-week shifts, patrolling seven nesting beaches and recording data on nesting females and nests. When a nest is vulnerable to surge or tidal flooding, the students relocate it to a safer place. In 2013, a satellite tagging program began that will help the project gather additional information about where these turtles come from and where they go after nesting at Guanahacabibes. The Ocean Foundation raises funds to purchase the satellite tags.

An ecological station run by the Cuban national parks system coordinates the sea turtle monitoring and protection. Staff offer guided sea turtle walks from June 25 to September 10 (mid-July to mid-August offers the best chances of seeing a nesting turtle). The walks, booked at the station visitor center, are limited to 10 people. The group waits quietly near one of the beaches until a nesting female has been spotted; then the guide leads everyone to watch her.

When tourists visit Guanahacabibes and its beaches, they can stay at Villa Maria la Gorda Hotel, which has a restaurant and dive shop, about 9 miles from the ecological station. In addition to some 30 dive sites accessed by boat, there is excellent snorkeling in the Bahia de Corrientes.

While Cuba in many ways outpaces other countries when it comes to conservation and sustainable practices, in many other ways it falls short. Public education and awareness of ecological issues are lacking, and shortages of personnel and resources hamper efforts. Despite the designation of Guanahacabibes as a protected area, no real protections exist. Tourism at Maria la Gorda and people on the beaches can represent a potential threat to the area's nesting sea turtles. Cigarette butts, toxic to turtles and other marine life, litter the beaches, and development here, while limited, is currently not practicing turtle-friendly lighting. Management of waste also presents a problem in such a remote area. If you go, follow turtle-friendly practices; take care not to disturb nesting turtles or nests. Do not leave any chairs or other items on the beach overnight or dig in or trample the sand. Avoid use of plastics, and pack out all trash. Dispose of cigarette butts properly.

More information:
Ocean Foundation: 202-887-8992, oceanfdn.org/blog/?p=752
Guanahacabibes National Park Ecological Station: 048-75-0366
    (international call), www.ecovida.pinar.cu/en/

How to help:
    Donate to the Ocean Foundation's conservation work in Cuba: oceanfdn.org/ocean-conservation-projects/listings/cuba-marine-research-and-conservation.

Other things to do in the area:
    Guanahacabibes Peninsula. The waters around the peninsula are a marine protected area known for many shallow scuba diving sites, including reefs and wrecks. The nature reserves have several trails: one leads to a cenote, or water-filled sinkhole; and another, to a cave system.

🐢 *Dominica*

The Dominica Sea Turtle Conservation Organization (DomSeTCO), established in 2007, promotes connections between science, policy, and public participation in the design and implementation of sea turtle research, conservation, and education in the Commonwealth of Dominica. DomSeTCO believes sustainable conservation must be nurtured from within, with strong community involvement, including the financial benefits of conserving the three remaining species of sea turtles there.

    The organization works with a variety of community organizations, groups, and individuals around Dominica, including Nature Enhancement Team at Rosalie; La Plaine Patrollers; North Eastern Wildlife Conservation, Environmental Protection and Tours (NEWCEPT); Mero Village Enhancement Committee; Layou Village Improvement Committee; Sunset Bay Hotel; Tamarind Tree Hotel; and Soufriere Scott's Head Marine Reserve. Its membership includes Forestry and Fisheries personnel, other public- and private-sector individuals, and the representative for Dominica from the Wider Caribbean Sea Turtle Conservation Network (WIDECAST). DomSeTCO relies on WIDECAST to provide the best available science for conservation and management. The University of the West Indies provides tagging equipment and tags.

The organization patrols nightly on three major nesting beaches—Bout Sable in La Plaine, Rosalie Beach, and Londonderry Beach—and has expanded over the years to include west coast and other beaches where both night and morning patrols are conducted. Some of these beaches have experienced the effects of climate extremes.

On the main Londonderry Beach and those extending from Hampstead to Melville Hall, members provide "Turtle Tours" to visitors from nearby hotels and guesthouses. A new Interpretation Welcome Centre serves as a base for the tours, as well as a central point where visitors can meet for tours, watch videos and presentations, and then go to the beach to see turtles once patrollers spot one.

The Interpretive Centre has restrooms and provides shelter for the patrollers during bad weather. The group sells souvenirs and refreshments there, providing an additional source of income. NEWCEPT has also conducted beach cleanups, some with nearby schools and communities.

More information:
Dominican Sea Turtle Conservation Organization, Inc.: 767-275-0724
    or 767-448-4091, https://facebook.com/pages/Dominica-Sea-
    Turtle-Conservation-Organization-DomSeTCO/114298085298885,
    domsetco@gmail.com or errolmar@cwdom.dm
Dominica Sea Turtle Hotlines: 767-616-8684 or 767-225-7742

How to help:
Donate to DomSeTCO through the WIDECAST website, widecast
.org (please indicate that the contribution is for DomSeTCO).

Olive ridley sea turtles.
(Photos by Guillaume Feuillet)

🏴 *Grenada*

Known as the Spice Island for its historic production of nutmeg, Grenada has many beaches and lush rain forest in the interior. It hosts one of the major nesting populations of leatherbacks, with 700 to 1,000 nests at Levera Beach, the main nesting site. Ocean Spirits, a nonprofit founded in 1999 and a member of WIDECAST, operates a conservation and research project here. Satellite tagging studies have shown that turtles nesting here travel as far as waters of the United Kingdom, West Africa, and Canada to feed. Local, trained guides conduct turtle watches for visitors on Levera Beach.

Ocean Spirits recruits volunteers for this project through Working Abroad. From March to August, become a research assistant for three weeks or more, taking part in nightly beach patrols, documenting and excavating nests and tagging leatherback sea turtles, or helping with community outreach programs on the island. You will stay in a house on the island, with single-sex bunk rooms, bath, and kitchen facilities. Everyone participates in preparing meals from seasonal, local produce and cheese.

More information:
Ocean Spirits: oceanspirits.org
Working Abroad: workingabroad.com/projects/ocean-spirits-sea-
    turtle-volunteer-programme-grenada-caribbean, Victoria.mcneil@
    workingabroad.com

How to help:
Donate cash or equipment to Ocean Spirits (see a list of needs on the website), or purchase Ocean Spirits gear. Click on "Support Us" at oceanspirits.org.

Other things to do in the area:
Levera National Park. Known for its beaches and lagoon, this park contains an abundance of waterfowl. You can snorkel over coral reefs and seagrass beds. Visit historic Carib's Leap, where in the 1600s, more than 40 Caribes leaped to their death to escape French troops; and the River Antoine Rum Distillery, the oldest on the island and only one in the Caribbean with a working water mill.

🪺 *Puerto Rico*

This island, a US territory, is one of the largest in the Caribbean. Green, leatherback, and hawksbill sea turtles nest and forage here, with loggerhead and olive ridleys seen on occasion. Protection under the US Endangered Species Act applies to Puerto Rico's sea turtles, which are also protected by Puerto Rican law. Two foraging grounds are federally designated critical habitats: one for greens at Culebra, an island 17 miles east of the main island of Puerto Rico about 7 miles long and 3.5 miles wide; and one for hawksbills at Mona Island, a rugged island nearly 50 miles west of the main island, actually closer to the Dominican Republic.

The Sea Turtle Program of Puerto Rico, which seeks to educate, investigate, recuperate, and protect the species, is a multiagency collaboration between Department of Natural and Environmental Resources; several nongovernmental organizations (NGOs); and other agencies, including WIDECAST, Sea Grant-University of Puerto Rico (UPR), Rio Piedras-UPR, Mayaguez-UPR, Chelonia, and Fish and Wildlife Service. WIDECAST brings together biologists, managers, community leaders, and educators in an effort to achieve sustainably managed sea turtle populations. It does this in part by facilitating and empowering local research and conservation programs in more than 40 wider Caribbean countries. Many of its projects are included in this section, as well as those on Central America and South America.

On several sites along the coast and on adjacent islands, nesting beach surveys are conducted, for leatherbacks April to July, and hawksbills August to December. Most leatherbacks nest in the Luquillo-Fajardo area and on Culebra Island. The most important hawksbill nesting beaches are at Mona Island and Humacao.

Maunabo

The town of Maunabo, on the southeastern coast, has three beaches: Playa Larga, Playa Maunabo (divided into two sectors, Bohíos and California), and Playa Emajaguas. Leatherbacks and hawksbills nest on these beaches. Amigos de las Tortugas Marinas (ATMAR) manages a community project that monitors and protects sea turtle nesting. The organization also provides community education and runs a volunteer program for Maunabo residents. Twenty-one locals participated in 2012, patrolling the beaches every morning during nesting season from March to November.

For visitors, ATMAR offers turtle walks from the Mauna Caribe Hotel, located on one of the nesting beaches, on Friday and Saturday nights from the last weekend of April to the first weekend of June, or peak nesting season. You do not have to be a guest at the hotel to participate, but tours are limited to 15 people, so reservations are recommended. To request a reservation, e-mail tortugasmaunabo@yahoo.com or call the hotel. There is no cost for tours, but donations are welcomed.

More information:
Amigos de las Tortugas Marinas: tortugasmaunabo.com (in Spanish)
Mauna Caribe Hotel: 787-861-3330, tropicalinnspr.com/
   paradormaunacaribe.php

How to help:
Make a donation at the beginning of a tour or via regular mail to Amigos de las Tortugas Marinas, HC-01 Box 2027, Maunabo, PR 00707.

Northeast Ecological Corridor

On the northeastern side of Puerto Rico, the communities of Luquillo and Fajardo adjoin Atlantic beaches where leatherback sea turtles nest from April through July. The adjacent El Yunque National Forest is a World Heritage Site and the country's second-most-visited spot. More than 3,000 acres around Luquillo were designated as a nature reserve, the Northeast Ecological Corridor, in 2008 by then-governor Aníbal Acevedo Vilá. In 2009, the next governor, Luis Fortuño, removed the designation in order to allow development in the area. A new governor, Alejandro García Padilla, was elected in 2013 and, thanks to the work of Sierra Club and other groups, restored protection of this area.

Little poaching occurs, but off-road vehicles pose a threat to nesting turtles and hatchlings, and unsustainable development represents a much greater threat. An annual Leatherback Festival takes place in April, and those interested in visiting this hard-to-reach area can call the local

Sierra Club about guided walks for individuals and groups, with at least a possibility of seeing crawl tracks or hatchlings in season.

The Luquillo Sunrise Beach Inn, located adjacent to one of the nesting beaches, keeps nesting tracking charts at the front desk. The inn offers daily beach walks into the Northeast Ecological Corridor to see flagged nesting sites and crawl tracks and, perhaps, to photograph emerging hatchlings.

More information:
Sierra Club: 787-688-6214, sierraclub.org/corridor/
Defenders of Northeast Ecological Corridor: facebook.com/
     corredorecologicodelnoreste (in Spanish)
Luquillo Sunrise Beach Inn: luquillosunrise.com/, facebook.com/
     luquillosunrise

How to help:
Avoid marked nests on the beach, and do not use flash photography or flashlights at night, as that could disorient hatchlings. Do not leave equipment on the beach overnight, and pack out all trash.

Other things to do in the area:
El Yunque Rain Forest. Explore the rain forest, which has hiking trails, informative signs, waterfalls, natural swimming pools, and lookout towers, all administered by the US Forest Service. Guided tours are available for views from the peak, at an elevation of 3,500 feet. Entry into the forest is free of charge, but the Visitor's Center costs $3.00 per person.
Kayaking. Kayak by moonlight through bioluminescent Fajardo Bay.
Water sports. Sailing, surfing, and snorkeling are also popular here.

🐢 St. Eustatius

This 5-mile-long and almost 2-mile-wide island is locally known as Statia. In Marine and Quill National Parks, volunteers who help sea turtle conservation serve in a variety of ways. During nesting season, March to October, volunteers help with a sea turtle conservation project for two weeks up to three months; beach patrols monitor and tag hawksbill,

A female leather-back returns to the sea in Grande Riviere, Trinidad.
(Photo by Brad Nahill/ SEEtheWILD)

green, and leatherback turtles under the supervision of resident interns from 9:00 p.m. to 3:00 a.m. (with time off the following morning). The island's nesting population is small, so patrols do not happen every night. Outside nesting season, qualified scuba divers may volunteer to help with in-water sea turtle surveys and observation in the park. Sea turtle monitoring began here on Zeelandia beach in 2002 and increased when the volunteer program began in 2003, with the first nesting leatherback observed in April of that year, followed by a number of others.

To volunteer for a few days or weeks, contact St. Eustatius National Parks (STENAPA), a nongovernmental, nonprofit foundation. Longer stints can be arranged through Working Abroad (the park is subject to government restrictions on length of service). After a four-day orientation, you work five days a week on the turtle project as well as in the botanical garden, on trails in the national park, and at the visitor center. During free time, you have the chance to explore, picnic, snorkel, swim, bird-watch, or just relax—or get scuba certified (additional cost) and dive in the marine park. Volunteers stay in designated campsites in the botanical garden at the base of a volcano. Bring your own camping gear, but bathrooms, showers, and cooking facilities are provided. You will receive an allowance for food, supplemented with fresh fruit from botanical garden trees and vegetables from the garden.

More information:
St. Eustatius National Parks: +599-318-2884 (international call), statiapark.org/volunteer/index.html
Working Abroad: workingabroad.com/page/28/statia-project-caribbean .htm, or info@workingabroad.com

How to help:
Support local tourism providers on the island. On the beach, follow turtle-friendly behaviors. Avoid single-use plastic items, and pack out all trash.

Other things to do in the area:
Attractions. The island attracts scuba divers, snorkelers, hikers, and those interested in colonial history.

🐢 *Trinidad and Tobago*

The Republic of Trinidad and Tobago, slightly smaller than the state of Delaware, includes two main islands in the southern Caribbean Sea. Independent since 1962, it is among the most prosperous of Caribbean nations thanks to oil and natural gas and, increasingly, tourism.

SOS Tobago

Tobago is the smaller of two main islands that make up the republic. Save Our Sea Turtles (SOS Tobago) aims to conserve Tobago's sea turtles and the coastal and marine habitat through research, education, and eco-tourism. SOS has managed a community-based project, focused on the leatherback and hawksbill sea turtles that nest on the island's beaches, in partnership with WIDECAST and Turtle Village Trust since 2000. From March to September each year, 10 to 20 volunteers patrol about 16 miles of beach to gather data, discourage poachers, and help hatchlings make the journey from nest to the sea. Volunteers receive training and stay in local eco-lodges or community-owned accommodations, with free time to explore the island's rich culture, beaches, coral reefs, and the oldest protected rain forest in the Western Hemisphere.

More information:
Save Our Sea Turtles: 868-328-7351 (international call), sos-tobago.org, facebook.com/SOSTobago, info@sos-tobago.org

How to help:
Adopt a turtle, volunteer, or make a donation at sos-tobago.org/how-you-can-help/adopt.

Other things to do in the area:
Explore the area. Snorkel, tour the rain forest, or explore historical and cultural sites.

Grande Riviere, Trinidad

A small, rural village along Trinidad's northern coast, Grande Riviere fronts one of the world's most important leatherback nesting beaches. Although less than a mile long, it hosts more than 5,000 turtles per season, and during peak season more than 500 turtles may nest in a single night. Some consider this beach to be the most densely nested by leatherbacks of any in the world.

As many as 15,000 people visit Grande Riviere each year, making it also one of the most-visited turtle beaches in the world. Ecotourism is key to the town's economy and conservation efforts, which are led by the Grande Riviere Nature Tour Guide Association. Two hotels are right on the beach (and both practice turtle-friendly lighting), meaning this beach is also one of the easiest places in the world to spot leatherbacks.

Leatherbacks nest from March to July, and hawksbills from May to September. To protect the sea turtles, Grande Riviere is a Forestry Division Prohibited Area, and a limited number of permits for turtle watching are distributed daily. Apply for turtle-watching permits at Forestry Division offices in Port of Spain, Sangre Grande, or San Fernando between the hours of 9:00 a.m. and 2:00 p.m., Monday to Friday (except on public holidays). Apply early to increase your chances of getting a permit. The Forestry Division recommends using one of the organizations currently authorized to conduct turtle walks here: Grande Riviere Nature Tour Guide Association and SOS Tobago.

More information:
Turtle Village Trust: turtlevillagetrust.org/turtle-watching.htm
SEEtheWILD: seeturtles.org/886/grande-riviere.html

How to help:
Visit nesting beaches with authorized guides only. Follow turtle-friendly practices while on the beach.

Matura, Trinidad

Matura is a rural village located near several rivers on the east-northeast shore of this southernmost Caribbean island. Two nearby beaches, Matura and Rincon, are protected, and during turtle nesting season, March to August, people are allowed on the beach only by permit. Nature Seekers facilitates conservation and education programs in Matura, giving residents and visitors the chance to volunteer alongside WIDE-

CAST scientists and staff from the Trinidad Forestry Division. Nature Seekers, established in 1990, reduced poaching of leatherback meat, eggs, and shells from 30 percent to zero, primarily by training the children of poachers as tour guides and reforestation workers.

Volunteers patrol the beaches; help guide tours; and weigh, measure, and tag turtles, providing data crucial to local and worldwide conservation efforts. In peak season, April to June, volunteers may see as many as 450 leatherbacks nest in one night, as well as some greens and hawksbills. Free time is available to hike to pristine Rio Seco waterfall, looking for parrots, toucans, and howler monkeys along the way, or to Mermaid Pools. Volunteers can also walk nature trails or kayak the lush Salybia River in their free time.

Earthwatch offers 12-day expeditions to volunteer with Nature Seekers in April, May, and June. Participants share double rooms with modern conveniences, including flush toilets and showers, in a guesthouse a 20-minute ride from the field site (the ride there offering great opportunity to watch for wildlife). Home-cooked meals of traditional Trinidadian fare are offered.

More information:
Nature Seekers: natureseekers.org
Earthwatch: earthwatch.org/exped/Sammy.htm

How to help:
Adopt a turtle, or make a donation to support conservation efforts: natureseekers.org/adopt-a-turtle/.

Other things to do in the area:
Explore the Matura area. Hike to the Rio Seco waterfall, kayak the Salybia River, or explore the village of Matura.

🐢 US Virgin Islands

The US Virgin Islands include St. Thomas, St. John, St. Croix, and several smaller islands. Three species of sea turtles nest and forage here: leatherback, hawksbill, and green. Loggerheads occasionally pass through the waters around the islands.

Buck Island Reef National Monument

Buck Island provides critical nesting habitat for hawksbill, loggerhead, leatherback, and green sea turtles. Hawksbills, the most endangered sea turtles in the eastern Caribbean, nest along the island's coastal beach forest. Roughly 40 to 60 females lay the majority of nests each season. Each year, from 10 to 20 greens nest above the sand berms and in the salt grass, one or two leatherbacks nest on open sand beach, and rarely, a loggerhead nests. Young sea turtles also rely on the area's seagrass and reef environments as feeding and developmental habitat.

The park is open year-round but closed from sunset to sunrise. Day trips to the National Monument (NM) are available from one of six National Park Service concessionaires on St. Croix, or you can use your own boat (anchoring permit required). Visitors to the island can enjoy the beach, called one of the 10 most secluded in the world; picnic; or hike up the narrow, steep overland trail through turpentine and pigeon-berry trees to the island's north reef overlook, returning to the beach down small switchbacks through organ pipe cactus and plumeria trees draped in hanging bromeliads. Snorkel an underwater trail to explore ancient elkhorn coral reef grottoes populated by a multitude of colorful reef fish. Two designated scuba moorings access 30- to 40-foot dives through haystack formations of elkhorn coral. Buck Island Reef NM contains the only elkhorn coral barrier reef in the US Caribbean. Snorkelers and divers may spot sea turtles foraging on reefs or in seagrass.

Visitors can volunteer at the National Park Service's Christiansted National Historic Site on St. Croix, and limited volunteer opportunities are available on Buck Island, depending on time of year and project activities.

More information:

Buck Island Reef National Monument: 340-773-1460, nps.gov/buis (find concessionaires under "Fees and Reservations")

Volunteer with the National Park Service: search by state or park at nps.gov/getinvolved/volunteer.htm

How to help:

Buck Island Reef NM became the first Marine Protected Area in the National Park System in 1961. No collecting of any kind is allowed. To protect fragile marine life, do not touch or stand on corals. Do not touch or feed fish or other wildlife.

☑ St. Croix, Jack & Isaac's Bay Preserve

The Nature Conservancy created the 301-acre Jack & Isaac's Bay Preserve in 1991 to protect nesting habitat for green and hawksbill sea turtles. At the time, about one-third of nests on these beaches fell into the hands of poachers, but monitoring and protection have reduced poaching to less than 1 percent. Staff, volunteers, and researchers patrol beaches during nesting season, monitor nesting females, remove invasive plants, and excavate hatched-out nests to release any hatchlings that did not make it out on their own.

The preserve generally accepts three volunteers each year to work the season from July through November. Volunteers work five days a week and help collect data on nesting females and, later in the season, on hatch success of nests and excavations. Housing is provided, and meals and some expenses are covered. Some background in science and some sea turtle experience are helpful. Apply for a volunteer position through the website nature.org/careers.

Visitors can take guided tours at night to watch turtles nesting and scientists collecting data. Later in the season, tours are held at sunset to watch nest excavations. A tour schedule is posted in early summer for approximately 10 tours in August and September. The beach is open all year, along with a display about the preserve and its natural resources. Tour fees help fund turtle monitoring and protection.

More information:
Jack & Isaac's Bay Preserve: 340-718-5575, nature.org/ourinitiatives/
 regions/caribbean/virginislands/usvi-protecting-sea-turtles-where-
 they-nest.xml

How to help:
Become a member of The Nature Conservancy, or donate directly to its efforts in the Virgin Islands at nature.org/ourinitiatives/regions/carib-bean/virginislands/giving/index.htm.

Leatherback hatchling. (Photo by Guillaume Feuillet)

Other things to do in the area:

Water sports. St. Croix is known for its white-sand beaches and also offers outstanding snorkeling and diving. An extensive, still mostly-healthy barrier reef, the largest of any in the Caribbean, surrounds the island. Other popular activities are boating, sailing, fishing, and kayaking.

Wildlife watching cruises. Wildlife watching cruises include those seeking humpback whales from February through April.

Hiking. Hikers can explore the island's rain forest and remote bays on their own or with guides.

A green sea turtle descends above the reef. (Photo by Scott Eanes)

Mexico

MEXICO boasts many miles of coastline, adjoining the Gulf of Mexico and Caribbean on its eastern side, and the Pacific Ocean and Sea of Cortez on its west. Along the Baja California peninsula, the world's longest, olive ridley, green, loggerhead, leatherback, and hawksbill sea turtles come to nest and to feed, some from as far away as Japan and Indonesia. The Sea of Cortez, or Gulf of California, a vibrant ocean rich in food sources and habitats, attracts olive ridleys and leatherbacks, which nest on its southern beaches. Sea turtles also nest on Gulf of Mexico beaches on Mexico's eastern coast and on those of the Caribbean along the Yucatán Peninsula and nearby islands.

In Mexico, as elsewhere, sea turtles face the threat of poachers, who eat or sell turtle meat and eggs on the black market, as well as degradation of habitat and loss of nesting beaches from coastal development. One of their biggest threats comes from fishing gear; sea turtles become entangled in fishing nets, trawls, and longlines and drown or sustain injuries that interfere with their ability to swim, eat, or reproduce.

🐢 Baja California Sur

Bahía Magdalena

On a secluded stretch of Isla Magdalena, a row of tents hidden among the sand dunes serves as base camp for RED Sustainable Travel's conservation adventures on Baja's Pacific coast (*red* means both "net," as in fishing net, and "network" in Spanish). Since 2000, local fishers and conservationists have monitored the sea turtle population in Bahía Magdalena, or Magdalena Bay, once a month, setting nets that they check every two hours for a 24-hour period to measure, weigh, and tag any turtles caught, then return them to the water. These data measure the effectiveness of efforts to help the endangered animals.

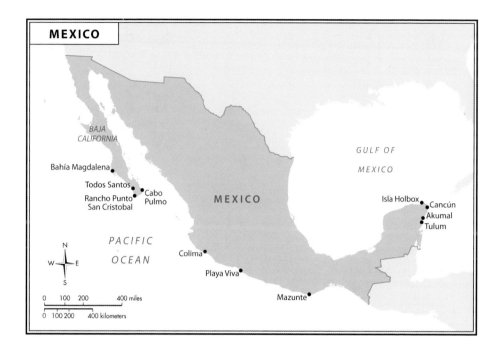

MEXICO

BAJA
CALIFORNIA

Bahía Magdalena

Todos Santos
Rancho Punto • Cabo
San Cristobal   Pulmo

PACIFIC
OCEAN

Colima

Playa Viva

Mazunte

MEXICO

GULF OF
MEXICO

Isla Holbox
Cancún
Akumal
Tulum

N
W   E
S

0   100   200   400 miles

0   100 200   400 kilometers

Grupo Tortuguero

S EA TURTLE conservation efforts in northwest Mexico took off in
    1998 with the formation of Grupo Tortuguero, or Turtler Group.
    Wallace J. Nichols and Jeffrey Seminoff, a marine ecologist and
leader of the Marine Turtle Ecology and Assessment Program with the
NOAA Fisheries Service, participated in its formation. This unlikely collection of fishers, scientists, conservationists, and community activists
created a grassroots network that today includes communities, organizations, agencies, institutions and hundreds of individuals. Thanks
to their hard work, most people living along the peninsula's coast
now understand that sea turtles are endangered and need protection.
Grupo Tortuguero performs in-water population monitoring and works

on nesting beach conservation, stranding assessment, reducing fishing bycatch, and carrying out research.

The group's philosophy centers on working within communities, engaging locals and empowering them as protectors of sea turtles— and supporting them in doing so. Gradually, this approach has changed centuries-old attitudes. Former poachers have become advocates for the turtles, and former fishers now work as ecotourism guides, sea turtle researchers, and conservationists. The organization's current field coordinator, Baja California Sur native Jesus "Chuy" Lucero, worked as a fisherman. But during a stint in Cabo Pulmo taking tourists snorkeling, diving, or sport fishing, he participated in a workshop on sea turtle conservation. Chuy then began participating in beach surveys and patrols and gradually became more involved in the organization before being named coordinator. Children, students, mothers, grandmothers, and teachers have joined in protecting the sea turtles and spreading the message of conservation.

Fishers, park staff, and local community members work with Grupo Tortuguero to monitor black sea turtle populations in Guerrero Negro, Punta Abreojos, Laguna San Ignacio, Mulege, Loreto, Agua Verde, San Carlos, Lopez Mateos, El Pardito, Desemboque, Punta Chueca, and Guasave. These local teams now have more than ten years of continuous data on the turtles, showing that area bays and estuaries deserve protection as critical feeding areas. The organization's work and research during the past 10 years also documented that small-scale local fisheries cause much of the loggerhead sea turtle mortality in the Pacific. Grupo Tortuguero and its partners are committed to working with government agencies and local communities to develop solutions that protect species and habitat and strengthen local economies. Many individuals work to bring together fishers here and around the world to reduce this mortality while preserving traditional livelihoods. You can help by purchasing only fish caught using turtle-friendly methods.

On the southern tip of Baja California, local organizations such as Amigos para la Conservación de Cabo Pulmo and Association for the Protection of the Environment and the Marine Turtle in Southern Baja (ASUPMATOMA) monitor beaches and protect nests. Travelers can volunteer with these local groups to help patrol beaches and report nests. Visit Grupo Tortuguero's Facebook page: facebook.com/grupo .tortuguero. ∎

In 2009, RED Sustainable Travel began supporting locals with training and business assistance, to create tourism opportunities out of conservation efforts. RED organizes trips that include camping, kayaking, and other adventures along with participation in Grupo Tortuguero's research. Allowing tourists to participate hands-on in the monitoring not only spreads the word about these efforts but also provides a sustainable employment option to local fishers. RED trips in Magdalena Bay provide 100 percent of the sea turtle monitoring costs, and in partnership with SEEtheWILD and other organizations, RED takes local youth on academic adventures to learn about mangroves, sea turtles, sand dunes, and sustainable fisheries.

Trips begin in La Paz, the capital of Baja California Sur and a vibrant seaside city. Explore the *malecón*, or seaside esplanade, and its many restaurants and shops, topped off with a fresh *raspada*, or shaved ice. Next day, the group travels by van across the peninsula to Mag Bay and, after an orientation to the area and its challenges, boards small boats called *pangas* for a ride through the bay to the camp.

Here, researchers place wide-weave, shallow nets across the path of the tide, and volunteers sign up for shifts to check the net throughout the night. The group also takes *panga* rides through lush mangroves to look for herons and egrets as well as kingfishers, jays, pelicans, osprey, and other birdlife. Hikes take the group over dunes towering more than four stories high and about a half a mile wide, which form a barrier between the bay and the Pacific Ocean, to a broad beach with no signs of civilization, to swim, relax, and explore.

One morning, head out with local fishers to learn about their sustainable methods, including hand lines, crab traps, and environmentally friendly slow shrimp trawls that skirt but do not drag the bottom. In camp, enjoy delicious meals of fresh, sustainable fish, shrimp, and clams, prepared by members of the cooperative.

In addition to financing the monthly monitoring project, these trips provide an alternative to typical tourism development (i.e., high-rise resorts, desert golf courses, and other eco-unfriendly options), creating dignified, meaningful work that keeps people in their communities.

SEEtheWILD also partners with RED on trips that include sea turtle monitoring with observing gray whales that give birth and raise their calves in Magdalena Bay in February and March. Small groups travel by *panga* with naturalist guides to search for whales, which often approach quite close to the small boats. RED offers occasional photo safaris as well, where you can learn alongside world-renowned nature photographers in majestic Magdalena Bay.

More information:
RED Sustainable Travel: redtravelmexico.com
SEEtheWILD: seethewild.org

How to help:
   Donate to Grupo Tortuguero or visit other areas where it operates: grupotortuguero.org.

Other things to do in the area:
   Isla Espíritu Santo. Visit this uninhabited island and UN Biosphere Preserve in the Sea of Cortez a short boat ride from La Paz.
   La Paz. Outfitters offer eco-adventures that include a safari camp on the beach, kayaking, hiking, and snorkeling with sea lions.

Cabo Pulmo

   The soft light of a half moon throws shadows from cacti onto the mountain slopes behind the beach and reflects off the dark sea before it. Waves hit the steep sand with impressive whumps, followed by the sigh of retreating water. There are no other lights as far as the eye can see, no other sound save that of feet on the sand. In Cabo Pulmo National Park, on the Sea of Cortez in Baja California Sur, vast stretches of beach still, astonishingly, remain largely untouched.
   The park, founded in 1995, takes in about 4 miles along the shore and extends 2.5 miles into the water, surrounding the sole hard coral reef in the Sea of Cortez, one of only three living reefs in western North America. With no park staff or enforcement, locals took it upon themselves to protect the natural resources on which their livelihoods had come to depend. In 2003, people of the village formed Amigos para la Conservación de Cabo Pulmo (ACCP), or Friends of Cabo Pulmo, primarily to protect sea turtles. The entire community helped. Local children painted signs marking boundaries of the park on the beach and encouraging turtle-friendly

behavior. Men descended from generations of fishers have become diving guides, and walls of the local dive shop sport photos of hatchling releases that involved everyone from four-year-olds to grandmothers. Visitors or locals who see the hatchlings, which fit easily in a child's palm, gamely swimming off into the wide-open water are not likely to forget the sight. An open depression in the sand surrounded by crumpled bits of leathery shells is also a hard image to shake. The abstract becomes personal, which reinforces the point.

In 2012, the community finalized a three-year effort—in cooperation with other NGOs, scientists and specialists, and Mexico's national parks administration, CONANP—to create a strategic plan for sustainable development, billing Cabo Pulmo as a "sanctuary of sea, land, and people, a truly ecological, rustic, and authentic destination."

Locals and park staff patrol three beaches—Playa Cabo Pulmo, Playa Los Frailes, and Playa Las Barraca—to search for olive ridley and green sea turtles coming ashore to nest and to check on previously marked nests. Even in this remote area, nesting turtles and eggs need protection from predators such as coyotes and feral dogs and from poachers. The need spans most of the year; ridleys, greens, and hawksbills nest from June until September or October, and nesting leatherbacks move onto the beaches from November to February, with eggs hatching between January and April. Visitors can help protect eggs from poachers and hatchlings from predators by simply being present.

In some cases, nests are protected in place. Workers remove the eggs, line the nest with fine mesh (to keep out crabs and digging animals), replace the eggs and sand, and cover it with a wire box, the openings small enough to keep out coyotes but large enough to allow hatchlings to escape. Ideally, someone will be present when those hatchlings emerge to shepherd them safely to the water. In other cases, eggs are taken to protected areas to incubate, and the hatchlings are later released on the same beaches where their eggs were laid.

More information:

Cabo Pulmo Sport Center: 52-624-1300235 (international call), cabopulmosportcenter.com

Cabo Pulmo National Park: pncabopulmo.conanp.gob.mx/ubicacion .php (in Spanish)

How to help:

If you see a nesting turtle, crawl tracks, or a suspected nest, report it to staff at the park kiosk or Cabo Pulmo Sport Center. Scuba divers can help by reporting sightings of sea turtles when diving in the park. Seek out and support locally owned, sustainable tourism such as that in Cabo Pulmo. Donate to ACCP at icfexchange.org/donateonline/?webkey=cabopulmo.

Other things to do in the area:

Cabo Pulmo. The village is a one-and-a-half-hour drive from the Cabo San Jose airport and about a three-hour drive from La Paz, the final 6 miles a serpentine unpaved road through cactus and scrub with tantalizing glimpses of the water until it finally tops a tall rise that affords a view of the entire village along the shore of endless blue sea. Streets in Cabo Pulmo lack names, but there are only two intersections, and everything is within easy walking distance. A small store stocks basics: canned goods; a smattering of produce, soft drinks, and candy bars; freshly made cheese; and the occasional fresh-baked muffins or cake. The town runs on solar power (and, unfortunately, a few generators). At night, enjoy the kind of dark city dwellers seldom experience and drink in a universe of stars before falling asleep to the sound of waves. There are bungalows and casitas for rent and several dive shops that offer snorkeling, fishing, and other activities. Snorkel Mermaid Cove, a sheltered pool on a swath of unsullied sand surrounded by huge boulders, or anywhere off the beach. Fish, bird, kayak, and in November through March, windsurf.

Los Barriles. This is a larger town with lodging, dining, shopping, and activities. Information on the Hotel Palmas de Cortez is available at 877-777-8862 or vanwormerresorts.com.

Rancho Punto San Cristobal

Across the cape on the Pacific coast, the private nonprofit Southern Baja California Association for the Protection of the Environment and the Marine Turtle (ASUPMATOMA) has coordinated sea turtle conservation efforts in the Los Cabos area since 1995. It is permitted to do research and protection from July to December along nearly 3 miles of Rancho Punto San Cristobal beach, which is accessed at Km 111 on Federal Highway 19 north of Cabo San Lucas, and 10 miles of Playa El Suspiro, accessed at Km 119 on the same highway. Olive ridley, leatherback, and occasionally green sea turtles nest here. As of the 2012 season, ASUPMATOMA had protected more than 7,000 nests, mostly olive ridleys, and released more than 560,000 hatchlings into the ocean.

Beginning July 15, visitors are allowed to come to the Rancho Punto San Cristobal sea turtle camp and observe mother turtles nesting, and beginning September 15, to witness and help with hatchling releases.

During nesting season, volunteers can help patrol six beaches, monitor nests, and release hatchlings. The rest of the year, volunteers are also needed to help prepare for and give workshops to teach local communities about sea turtle conservation and to help with general preparation and maintenance. Volunteers are asked to commit to one month and live in camp facilities at Rancho Punto San Cristobal at Km 111 on the Cabo San Lucas highway. It has hot water and electricity but no Internet service; food is not provided, but a kitchen is available.

More information:
ASUPMATOMA: 52-624-1430269 (international call), asupmatoma.org
    (in Spanish), asupmatoma@hotmail.com

How to help:
Patronize locally owned businesses whenever possible, and let your hosts know that you traveled here to see sea turtles.

Todos Santos

About a 40-minute drive north of Cabo San Lucas, the village of Todos Santos attracts the arts crowd as well as surfers and beach lovers. One of the town's most famous establishments is Hotel California, a dozen colorful rooms in a historic, two-story building, each of them different. Some overlook a dark blue pool; others have private patios or open onto a veranda above the main avenue, the better to enjoy temperate weather afforded by the town's location on an underground stream in foothills overlooking the Pacific.

Olive ridley, leatherback, and black sea turtles (black sea turtles are a variant of the green sea turtle) nest on nearby beaches. From October through April, a local organization, Tortugueros Las Playitas, brings in volunteers to work with biologists and technicians to patrol for nests, relocate eggs, manage the incubation area, and help release hatchlings. Other volunteer opportunities are available the rest of the year. Volunteers work 4 to 10 hours a day, with time off to explore Todos Santos and environs. Casitas at La Sirena Eco-Adventures, the starting and ending point for beach patrols, include queen beds, private bathrooms, cable TV and Wi-Fi, with a large semi-outdoor kitchen—all just a few blocks from the town center.

More information:
Tortugueros Las Playitas: 213-265-9943, todostortugueros.org

How to help:
In addition to volunteering with Tortugueros Las Playitas, you can make a donation, adopt a nest, or adopt a hatchling on the website.

Colima

Projects Abroad operates a sea turtle conservation project at Campamento Tecoman, a three-hour drive from Guadalajara on an 18-mile beach where olive ridleys nest. Volunteers work with trained staff on night beach patrols, collecting turtle eggs and placing them in a protected corral, and helping hatchlings that emerge from nests in the corral to reach the sea. Volunteers also spend one day a week at the project's crocodile farm helping prepare food, collecting data, and doing general maintenance, and one day on a biodiversity project in the lagoon, learning to identify birds and recording data.

Volunteers normally work about five hours each day, mainly on one of two night shifts, from 10:00 p.m. to 3:00 a.m. or 3:00 a.m. to 8:00 a.m., patrolling the beach and bringing eggs into the protected area. The rest of the day is free for relaxing, exploring, and enjoying the beach. There are turtles here year-round, but the busy season runs June to December. In the slower months, January to May, volunteers may help extend the corral (the protected area where eggs are reburied) or go along on boat trips to monitor marine wildlife such as whales and dolphins. Volunteers stay in

RED: Conservation and Community

UNLIKE MANY in conservation, Chris Pesenti is not a biologist, does not hold a science degree, and is not a lawyer. But his skills include the ability to drink beer with fishermen, learn how to make goat's milk cheese from an *ama de casa* (homemaker), tag and release sea turtles, and work with Mexican government officials to devise forward-thinking development strategies.

Pesenti, who first got to know the Baja California peninsula as a teen slipping over the border to surf with his buddies, helped to found or strengthen a half-dozen conservation organizations, including ProPeninsula, Grupo Tortuguero, Guardianes del Aqua de La Paz, Vigilantes de Bahía Magdalena, Loreto Baykeeper, and Amigos para la Conservación de Cabo Pulmo.

His first such effort was ProPeninsula, an NGO aimed at strengthening grassroots conservation efforts, which he founded as part of his thesis for a master's degree in international relations and Pacific studies from the University of California–San Diego. Pesenti based the organization on his realization that long-term conservation depended not on professionals and large NGOs but local leaders and members of communities.

During the course of a decade, Pesenti mentored a new generation of unlikely leaders, including an ex-poacher, filmmaker, college student, scientist, concerned mother, and retired businesswoman, eventually launching a network of conservation organizations in communities throughout Baja California Sur that remains active. Throughout the process, he realized that the model—while successful in raising awareness throughout the region and creating a network of local partners to stand up for their community and environment—was incomplete.

In 2009, he launched RED Sustainable Travel, seeking to link preservation of species and habitat with economic development through tourism. RED creates authentic experiences that make travelers part of the conservation effort. Their hosts, more than just wage earners, are the men and women who are either directly hired and trained by RED or the owner-operators of small community businesses that are part of

RED's program to support businesses in rural communities. This kind of tourism offers a unique experience and a way to contribute directly to conservation and local communities, supporting activities such as sea turtle monitoring and community environmental education. The experience is a two-way street; many of the local participants were involved in practices harmful to the environment—poaching, overfishing, and harvesting sea turtles. Now they are tourism providers who value natural resources.

"We want the fishermen to keep fishing and, at the same time, raise their level of consciousness," Pesenti says. "That's who they are, and the close relationship they have with the sea is essential to conservation in the long-term. They want to invite tourism into their community but in a responsible manner that enhances and preserves their way of life. At the same time, travelers get a hands-on look into their culture, into a lifestyle handed down since the Jesuits came to the peninsula.

"If families are worried about what's on the table, in the bank, or the roof over their head," he adds, "it's tough to ask them to think about species and habitat conservation. That's why it is essential to link economic development to conservation. Creating local stewards is crucial to preserving some of the last truly wild places on the Baja California peninsula. These complex issues require all the tools we have available."

As an example, he points to a man who lives in Magdalena Bay and does some fishing. "Let's call him 'H.' Without really knowing what RED was all about," Pesenti said, "'H' became a chef in the tourism cooperative in Magdalena Bay. After one of the first trips 'H' pulled me aside and asked me how long we had been working together. Four months, I responded, and he then took a deep breath and said, 'Okay, four months and two weeks ago, I prepared sea turtle for a *caguamada*.' It turns out that he was known as the guy in town to prepare sea turtle dishes. He knew where to get it, how to prepare it, and he was well known throughout the region for his talents. Remember that sea turtles are endangered and protected by law in Mexico. Then 'H' added, 'I get it now; I understand why we are doing this.' He saw how important it was for the tourists to see and touch the sea turtles and vowed to never again cook sea turtle. On a later trip, 'H' brought his son to the campsite to witness the sea turtle monitoring and learn why it is important. He has become a positive example in his community, no small feat here." ■

basic dormitory-style bunkhouses and have lunch, the main meal of the day, provided by a local cook. Food is provided in the kitchen for making breakfast and dinner. The ideal time period to volunteer is one month, but the project accepts volunteers for a shorter time period.

Every few days, groups travel into the local town for Internet access and to buy a few luxuries such as chocolate. Occasional weekend trips away from the camp give everyone a well-earned break.

More information:
Projects Abroad: 888-839-3535, projects-abroad.org/volunteer-projects/
    conservation-and-environment/volunteer-mexico/

How to help:
If you cannot volunteer, you can help someone else do so. Projects Abroad volunteers often need help raising money to fund the experience. Call Projects Abroad (888-839-3535) to see how you can donate to sponsor a volunteer.

Guerrero

Playa Viva

Playa Viva, a luxury eco-resort in Juluchuca on the Pacific coast of Mexico about 30 minutes south of Zihuatanejo, is home to a turtle sanctuary established by locals. Thousands of green and dozens of leatherback sea turtles nest here year-round, with peak nesting during the rainy season between May and September. An all-volunteer staff from the local community took on the name La Tortuga Viva (The Living Turtle), obtained training from the Mexican Department for the Protection of Endangered Species, and set up camp at the edge of an estuary close to the nesting beach. In 2010, their team protected more than 100,000 turtle eggs.

Guests at the eco-resort can join La Tortuga Viva on night beach patrols to search for tracks and nesting greens and to help transport eggs to an incubation pen in the sanctuary. Mornings, guests can help collect hatchlings and release them down the beach. Playa Viva provides vehicles and supplies for the turtle camp and food stipends for the local volunteer staff. The lands around the resort, used for permaculture and organic farming for the community and resort dining facilities, include 160 acres of private nature reserve that provide opportunities to hike and bird-watch.

More information:
Playa Viva: playaviva.com

How to help:
Make a donation designated for Friends of la Tortuga Viva through the Ocean Foundation: oceanfdn.org/donate?friend=la-tortuga-viva.

🏴 *Oaxaca*

Mazunte

In the 1950s, an estimated 10 million olive ridleys nested each year on Mexico's southern Pacific coast. By 1988, that number had plummeted to around 40,000 because of wholesale slaughter of the turtles for meat and other products. At a slaughterhouse in San Agustín, on the coast of the state of Oaxaca between the village of Mazunte and the town of Puerto Angel, more than 30,000 turtles were killed each year between 1968 and 1990. In 1990, the Mexican government banned harvest of all species of sea turtles throughout the country. Today, on nearby Escobilla Beach, *arribadas* of tens of thousands of olive ridleys occur, an encouraging turnaround.

In 1994, the Mexican Turtle Center opened in Mazunte. Its large main building houses an aquarium with five species of sea turtles as well as representatives of many other types of turtles found in the area. During the nesting season, the center works with the local community to guard nests on Escobilla and to release hatchlings. Visitors can participate in both activities.

More information:
Mexican Turtle Center: centromexicanodelatortuga.org/ (in Spanish)

How to help:
Purchase locally made souvenirs at the Mexican Turtle Center.

📑 *Quintana Roo*

The Mexican state of Quintana Roo occupies the eastern half of the Yucatán Peninsula and includes nearly 80 miles of Caribbean Sea coastline. Green, loggerhead, hawksbill, and leatherback sea turtles nest on these beaches; and green, loggerhead, hawksbill, and Kemp's ridley travel through and forage in these waters.

Akumal

Akumal, which means "place of the turtles" in Mayan, is a wide bay between Playa del Carmen and Tulum. A 20-year-old sea turtle conservation program here is run by the Ecological Center of Akumal (CEA), which also has projects on marine ecosystems and water quality. CEA monitors 3 miles of beach for nesting loggerhead and green sea turtles and needs volunteers, especially from August to October.

Volunteers must commit to at least one month. In addition to monitoring nesting beaches, recording data, and protecting nests, they may help monitor juvenile green sea turtles that forage in the bay, monitor the behavior of visitors snorkeling in the bay, or attend sea turtle talks on hotel-front beaches. There is a small fee for dorm-style housing near the

---

How Conservation Tourism Helps in Mexico (and Everywhere Else)

Providing tour-guiding and other ecotourism-related services offers an alternative to fishing, which accidentally catches thousands of turtles every year in this region.

▶ Establishing small-scale tourism companies in more remote areas creates local support for efforts to protect important habitat from unsustainable coastal development.
▶ Income from travelers who come to watch sea turtles helps fund conservation and research efforts. ■

beach, as well as access to a common kitchen and discounts at many area restaurants. Volunteers must be at least 19 years of age. During time off, volunteers relax or enjoy the Akumal beach, snorkeling, and diving.

Outside nesting season, volunteers can help with public education programs (speaking English is a plus), community outreach and school programs (Spanish required), carpentry, office work, graphic design, and bird counts, and other research projects. The project could even use volunteers to teach English to the staff.

Several tour operators offer guided snorkel tours in the bay. These are limited to 10 people, and an orientation is required in an effort to minimize the effects of this activity on the foraging greens and other marine life.

More information:
Ecological Center of Akumal: ceakumal.org
To volunteer: Fill out an online application form (available seasonally) at
   ceakumal.org/html_en/volunteers/application_forms.php or contact
   tortugas1@ceakumal.org

How to help:
Adopt a turtle, nest, or family during the season at ceakumal.org/html_en/want_to_help/adoptions.php. Make a donation to or become a member of CEA.

Other things to do in the area:
Snorkeling and diving. Take a snorkel tour of the bay or a cenote; snorkel at night; or dive reefs a short boat ride away with Akumal Dive Shop. The shop also offers lionfish hunting excursions for divers, which include cleaning your catch and delivering it to the chef at a nearby restaurant, who will prepare it for your dinner. Contact Akumal Dive Shop at akumaldiveshop.com.

Cancún Hotel Projects

Swanky high-rise hotels line the beach of Cancún, the most developed part of the Yucatán Peninsula. Yet hundreds of sea turtles nest here from

May through November—a total of 5,600 nests were laid in 2012—and the municipality's Department of Ecology is charged with their protection. Ninety percent of area hotels cooperate with the program, moving furniture from the beach at night, turning off lights, and relocating nests to safer areas on their beachfront. Signs marking the protected nest areas educate tourists about sea turtle nesting. The department provides instructions for hotel personnel on what to do when a sea turtle nests on the beach, how to transfer eggs safely and build a nesting barrier, what precautions to take, and how to ensure the well-being of nesting adults and hatchlings. Field supervisors help with patrols and egg transfers, and patrol opportunities are available to volunteers, who receive training.

Agency and hotel staff patrol Isla de Cancún beaches nightly, and the agency has a 24-hour hotline for people to call if they see a nesting turtle or nest. These hotels also invite guests to participate in hatchling releases in late evening. In most cases, individuals are handed a baby sea turtle to physically release. Many scientists consider such handling of these endangered animals a bad idea (it is illegal in the United States). On the other hand, this kind of up close and personal experience with sea turtles can be a life-changing experience for tourists who previously knew little or nothing about sea turtles or the environment. If you participate in a program that involves direct contact with sea turtles, wash your hands before and after handling the animals, for their protection and yours.

The Ritz-Carlton Cancun began a turtle program in 2002; members of the hotel staff volunteer for nightly patrols of the beach in front of the hotel, and guests can volunteer as well. Guests can also sign up with the concierge to receive a phone call if a nesting turtle is spotted, so they can go out to the beach and witness it. As many as 20 sea turtles have nested in one night in front of the hotel, with a total of 235 in 2012. Guests are invited to nighttime hatchling releases.

Palace Resorts properties, which include Moon Palace Resort, Le Blanc Spa Resort, Beach Palace, and Sun Palace, participate in the program as well. From the 2006 to 2012 seasons, turtle camps at these hotels brought in a total of 8,181 nests and released 739,331 hatchlings, mostly green with some loggerhead and fewer hawksbills.

All hotels participating in the program keep records of the number of nests, species of sea turtle, number of eggs, and hatching success and report it to the agency.

Three area Sandos hotels have a Sandos Ecoclub that works with the appropriate sea turtle conservation program. On the beach in front of the Sandos Cancun hotel, 41 nests were protected in 2012 and 4,423 hatchlings released. Although its numbers are much smaller (5 nests in 2012), Sandos Caracol Eco-Resort in the Riviera Maya also operates a program on its beach, moving furniture in at night and placing nests in a protected area. This location has a variety of environmental education programs. Guests can view displays and attend talks on sea turtles and other aspects of the natural world in this area in the resort's Eco-Club room. Sandos Playacar reported a leatherback turtle on its beach in 2012.

In the best-case scenario, we would not build hotels, homes, or businesses on beaches where sea turtles nest. However, people love the beach, companies around the world make a lot of money from tourist development on the coast, and hotels already occupy many of these beaches. The next best thing is for property owners, businesses, and hotels to be aware of the needs of the sea turtles and to do all they can to minimize the negative effects. Programs such as Cancún's, while not perfect, are at least an effort and may reach many people who otherwise would never have a sea turtle experience. If you visit, ask whether a hotel participates in the program to protect sea turtles before staying there. Report any inappropriate actions that you see to the program's director of ecology at ecologica@cancun.gob.mx.

More information:
Benito Juárez Department of Ecology: 044-998-881-2800, ext. 2269; after-hours hotline, 044-998-155-9939 (international calls)
Sandos Caracol and Sandos Cancun: sandos.com/hotels-in-mexico.htm
Ritz-Carlton Cancun: http://www.ritzcarlton.com/en/Properties/Cancun/Default.htm

Isla Holbox

This island lies a 30-minute boat ride from Chiquila, which is about two hours by car from Cancún. Many Cancún hotels can arrange day trips to the island. From April to October, green, hawksbill, loggerhead, and leatherbacks nest on 14 miles of beach from Punta Mosquito to Caba Catoche on the northwestern side of a cape adjacent to Holbox. An NGO called ProNatura has the permit to protect and monitor nesting on this beach.

Volunteers stay in a common house on Holbox, which has a kitchen, and travel to the nesting beach by boat each night to patrol for nests. Volunteers leave nests in place, marking the site and recording GPS coordinates along with species and date. They will move nests that appear to be in vulnerable areas. Volunteers then return to nests at the appropriate time and record hatching success.

Patrols are generally canceled when the weather is bad, as this makes travel by boat difficult, but there is talk of establishing camps on the beach so that volunteers can conduct patrols every night. Before the volunteer program started, locals camped on both ends of the beach during the season and did continuous monitoring. This continuous presence not only created a more complete set of data but gave the turtles greater protection from poaching and predators such as raccoons. If volunteers express interest in establishing camps at the nesting beach, ProNatura may do so. Volunteers must commit for at least one month and get three days off each month to enjoy activities on Holbox.

ProNatura's main office in Merida assigns volunteers to turtle camps on the northern side of Quintana Roo and the neighboring state of Campeche, based on need. Outside nesting season, volunteers can help with other ProNatura projects.

More information:
ProNatura: pronatura.org.mx (in Spanish)
To volunteer, register and fill out an application: pronatura.org.mx/
    voluntariado/

Other things to do in the area:
   Isla Holbox. Isla Holbox is famous for its lobster pizza. Try one!
   Whale Shark Biosphere Preserve. Swim with whale sharks in waters north of the island. The largest fish in the world, these enormous sharks are tranquil filter feeders. Guided tours are offered by V.I.P. Holbox Experience: vipholbox.com.
   Crocodile Preserve. Sign up for a boat tour, snorkel outing, or fishing trip.

Riviera Maya and Tulum Sea Turtle Conservation Program

The area from Puerto Morelos, just south of Cancún, roughly 75 miles to the Sian Ka'an Biosphere Reserve, is known as the Riviera Maya. Flora, Fauna y Cultura, an NGO, manages the Riviera Maya and Tulum Sea Turtle Conservation Program, monitoring and protecting nesting on 13 beaches. The project operates through six turtle camps: Aventuras-DIF, Xcacel, Xel-Há, Tankah, and Kanzul and Lirios Balandrín, with the support of Xcaret, which also operates a sea turtle hospital and educational programs (read more about the Xcaret facility in the Captive Encounters section). In 2012, the project released a total of 700,000 hatchlings.

Project staff and volunteers conduct patrols on these beaches during nesting season. They leave most nests in place on the beach, marking the nest and recording the type of turtle, date, and other data. Sometimes they relocate eggs into a human-made nest near the original one if, for example, the nest lies in a low area or right at the bottom of access stairs. They also sometimes move nests from highly developed beaches to hatcheries, later releasing them on more natural beaches. In certain cases, for example, when the threat of a hurricane is imminent, eggs that have been incubating for at least 40 days will be removed from nests, placed in boxes, and transported to a safe area.

Flora, Fauna y Cultura offers guided nesting tours from June through September and hatchling release tours from August through October on Xcacel beach. Both tours are limited to small groups, and reservations are recommended. Tours start with an orientation and instructions for participation, take place at night, and may require walking long distances or in the rain. Wear dark clothing and comfortable shoes, and do not bring flashlights or flash cameras.

The project accepts volunteers for a minimum commitment of one month. Volunteers live in a former restaurant at Xcacel, which has several large bunk rooms, lockers, and a common kitchen right next to the beautiful, white-sand beach. Nesting season runs from May to mid-November, and during the off-season, volunteers can help with education, outreach, and even making sea turtle crafts that are sold at area hotels. Flora, Fauna y Cultura is working with hotels and resorts to educate tourists about sea turtles, how tourism and other activities affect them, and how people can reduce the negative effects. The program also works to educate communities about sea turtles and their importance to the local economy.

Two of the project's beaches lie within the Sian Ka'an Biosphere Reserve. Established in 1986, this protected area is part of UNESCO's Man and the Biosphere program and a UNESCO World Heritage Site. Sian Ka'an, which in Mayan means "birth of the sky," encompasses approximately 1.3 million acres and 75 miles of Mexico's Caribbean coastline, almost a third of its total length, and takes in two important nesting areas.

Volunteers at the Sian Ka'an location stay and work at the Ecological Center of Sian Ka'an, which goes by the Spanish acronym CESIAK. The center lies down a road winding through Tulum town, through several miles of casitas, eco-hotels, restaurants, and camps packed on either side of the narrow pavement, which then turns to sand. CESIAK monitors Kanzul beach just before the entrance to Sian Ka'an, Campechen beach from the entrance to the center, and Lirios Balandrín around the center, each of them almost 3 miles long.

As a volunteer, you will stay in beachfront tent cabins without electricity but with access to a main building that has electricity, Internet access, bathrooms, showers, and a restaurant that provides volunteers with meals. Every night, you will patrol 5.5 miles of beach for nesting sea turtles. You may also conduct turtle walks or hatchling releases for visitors to the preserve. Volunteer positions always fill up during nesting season, and it helps to speak English and have some knowledge of sea turtles or conservation. However, there are other volunteer opportunities available during the off-season. Volunteers at Sian Ka'an must commit to a minimum of one month because of the training needed. You will get a day off each week and can enjoy excursions in the preserve or explore nearby Tulum and the Riviera Maya.

You can also visit Sian Ka'an on a SEEtheWILD whale shark and sea turtle trip, offered June through August, when whale sharks congregate off the Yucatán coast to feed on seasonal plankton upwellings. The expedition starts on Isla Mujeres for two days of excursions to see gentle, plankton-eating whale sharks, the world's largest fish. Travel by boat with 10 people maximum, departing each morning to search for whale sharks and returning by 1:00 or 2:00 p.m. for lunch. Afternoons will be free to explore the island and surrounding waters. You will spend three nights in the eco-lodge at Sian Ka'an and visit Mayan archeological sites, experience an authentic Mayan lunch, take a boat ride in the lagoon, and swim in the river. You will take a night walk to look for nesting turtles on the green sea turtle nesting beach at Xcacel with a guide from Flora, Fauna y Cultura.

The trip concludes with a Punta Allen Eco-adventure tour of the most-preserved portion of the Yucatán Peninsula's coral reef, including a boat ride through the lagoons, where you may see manatees or some of the 353 species of birds living here, with a stop on a mangrove island and at a cenote, one of the freshwater limestone lagoons scattered across the peninsula. Once at Punta Allen, you will learn about the community's conservation-oriented way of life, hike, and snorkel over the coral reef. A portion of your trip fee goes to Flora, Fauna y Cultura.

More information:
Flora, Fauna y Cultura: 01-984-87152-44 (international call),
    florafaunaycultura.org (in Spanish)
To volunteer: contact Carolin Hohenegger, 01-984-871-52-44
    (international call), Sumate1@florafaunaycultura.org
SEEtheWILD: seethewild.org/541/41/yucatan-sea_turtles-whale_
    sharks-mexico.html
Sian Ka'an Biosphere Reserve: whc.unesco.org/en/list/410
CESIAK: cesiak.com.mx (in Spanish)
Volunteer in Sian Ka'an Biosphere Reserve for as little as two
    weeks with Global Vision International: gviusa.com/programs/
    volunteer-turtles-mexico

How to help:
Make a donation to Flora, Fauna y Cultura. If you stay at area hotels, let them know you are interested in sea turtles and the programs offered by the organization. Whenever possible, stay in locally owned hotels and those with eco-friendly practices. Hire local guide services.

Other things to do in the area:
Grand Cenote. Dive or snorkel the cenote with Xibalba Dive Center in Tulum, just a few minutes from the cenote: http://xibalbahotel.com/diving.asp.

Tip: Reducing Plastic Use While Traveling

In remote and still-developing areas, trash becomes more than an eyesore; it can threaten the health and even survival of wildlife. Single-use plastic items such as water bottles are a particular problem because they last a long time (and never really go away, breaking down into smaller and smaller pieces until becoming essentially plastic dust) and can travel long distances on water and wind. Reducing the amount of trash we produce can seem especially difficult when we travel. Here are some tips to help you cut down on plastic waste.

▶ Carry refillable water bottles. Take them through airport security empty, and then fill them up at a water fountain. If you are traveling in a country where the tap water is not safe to drink, ask to have them filled with purified water in the hotel restaurant or purchase one large bottle of water and use it to refill your reusable ones. Rinse your bottle frequently, and occasionally let it dry out completely.

▶ Bring reusable tote bags for shopping and restaurant takeout. Wash these occasionally. Despite alarming news reports, reusable bags are unlikely to make you sick. The one study that these reports continue to cite was funded by the American Chemistry Council, which represents makers of single-use plastic bags. While the study noted "large numbers of bacteria" on the bags, there are large numbers of bacteria all around us, including in and on our bodies. Those researchers found *E. coli*, a potentially harmful bacteria, on only 12 percent of the bags; after adding meat juices and leaving bags in a car trunk for two hours, the bacteria increased 10-fold. This bit of artificially induced risk is what most news reports seem to focus on, creating a widespread belief that reusable bags will make us all ill. The study report admits that washing bags reduced the bacteria by more than 99.9 percent. Of course, if you carry nonfood items, you have even less to worry about, and the sea turtles will thank you.

▶ Purchase travel-sized containers, and carry your own shampoo, conditioner, and lotion so you will not need to use the small, disposable bottles in your hotel room.

▶ Bring a reusable drink cup, so when you are enjoying beverages on a hotel beach, you can refill the cup rather than use a new plastic one each time. A reusable coffee mug helps cut down on plastic waste, too. Pack these in your suitcase with socks or other items inside them to save space. ■

PacChen. Have an authentic Mayan experience at PacChen, kayaking across a lagoon and hiking through jungle to see spider monkeys, then enjoying a traditional Mayan lunch. Or rappel into a cenote, hike up to the rim and zipline across, swim in an underground cenote, and have a traditional meal at Tres Reyes. Contact Alltournative at alltournative .com.

Mayan Pottery Workshop. Near the Mayan ruins at Coba, visit a Mayan pottery workshop: loltun.net (in Spanish).

Researchers finish collecting information from a nesting leatherback in Cahuita, Costa Rica.
(Photo © Neil Ever Osborne; www.neileverosborne.com)

Central America

⚑ *Costa Rica*

THIS CENTRAL AMERICAN nation abuts both the Caribbean Sea and the Pacific Ocean and contains some of the most active nesting beaches in the world. Costa Rica is considered by many to be the birthplace of ecotourism, although its image as an environmentally friendly country was somewhat tarnished by controversies over potential downgrading of national parks and attempted unsustainable development by foreign countries. Ultimately, that did not happen, and not only did sea turtle conservation projects using beach patrols, volunteers, and ecotourism begin here but Costa Rica remains a hotbed of efforts to save sea turtles.

Costa Rica's Caribbean coast is one of the most important leatherback nesting grounds in the world, and more green turtles nest here than anywhere else in the Western Hemisphere. The Pacific coast contains some of the world's most important olive ridley nesting sites.

Continuing threats to sea turtles here include human consumption of turtle eggs and meat, incidental capture in fishing gear, plastic pollution, and development. Sea turtle eggs are considered a delicacy, and some still see them as an aphrodisiac, which supports an active black market.

Cahuita National Park

This park protects the country's largest coral reef and includes one of its most beautiful beaches. Ecotourism based on the hawksbill and leatherback sea turtles that nest seasonally here is the focus of a community-based project managed by the Latin American office of the Wider Caribbean Sea Turtle Conservation Network (WIDECAST). This organization brings together biologists, managers, community leaders, and

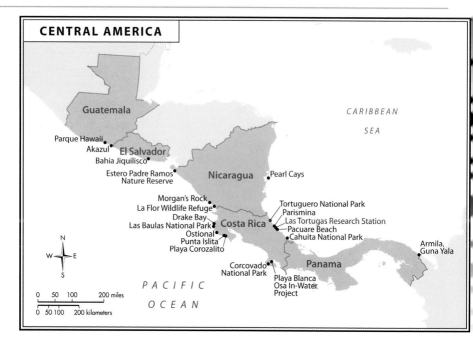

CENTRAL AMERICA

Guatemala

CARIBBEAN

SEA

Parque Hawaii
Akazul
El Salvador
Bahia Jiquilisco

Estero Padre Ramos
Nature Reserve

Nicaragua

Pearl Cays

Morgan's Rock
La Flor Wildlife Refuge
Drake Bay
Las Baulas National Park
Costa Rica
Ostional
Punta Islita
Playa Corozalito

Tortuguero National Park
Parismina
Las Tortugas Research Station
Pacuare Beach
Cahuita National Park

Armila,
Guna Yala

Corcovado
National Park

Panama

Playa Blanca
Osa In-Water
Project

PACIFIC

OCEAN

N
W — E
S

0   50 100   200 miles

0 50 100   200 kilometers

educators in an effort to achieve sustainably managed sea turtle populations. It does this in part by facilitating and empowering local research
and conservation programs in more than 40 other Caribbean countries.
Cahuita, one of five such projects in Costa Rica, began in 2000 and has
reduced egg take, once an estimated 90 percent, to less than 20 percent,
even as the population has grown and improved roads have made access
easier.

From March to October each year, 20 to 30 volunteers are accepted
to help patrol 5 miles of nesting beach, gather data, keep poachers away,
and help hatchlings safely make the journey from nest to surf. Volunteers
receive training and stay in a local eco-lodge or community-owned cabin.
Free time is available to visit an iguana farm and botanical garden, hike in
the rain forest, or enjoy the beach and ocean.

More information:
WIDECAST: 506-2241-7431 (international call),
   latinamericanseaturtles.org

How to help:

Adopt a hatchling, adult turtle, nest, or section of the beach or donate something on the organization's wish list.

Corcovado National Park, Osa Peninsula

The Osa Peninsula contains the largest single expanse of lowland tropical forest in Central America. Corcovado National Park offers camping at three ranger stations, two of which are on the coast: La Leona on the park's southern tip, and San Padrillo on the northern end, near Corcovado beach's nearly 12 miles of uninterrupted sand. The headquarters and research center of this remote and mostly undeveloped park are located at Sirena on the Pacific coast deep inside the park. There are also cabins at La Leona, and a trail connects it with Sirena, about 13 miles away. In addition to 4 species of sea turtles, the park protects more than 100 species of mammals, including monkeys, sloths, and anteaters, and nearly 400 species of birds, including scarlet macaws and resplendent quetzals. For those willing to rough it, this place gets you close to nature.

On Piro and Pejeperro beaches south of the park, Osa Conservation operates a sea turtle program that accepts volunteers July through November. Commit to a minimum of one week, working 30 hours, and participate in nightly and morning beach surveys, measuring and recording data on sea turtles, tagging turtles, monitoring nesting sites, and relocating eggs to a hatchery. Volunteers stay in facilities in Piro Biological Station, which backs up to lush rain forest and offers extensive hiking trails. You will be immersed in the local culture, community, and natural environment yet will be completely comfortable. There is a program fee and a lodging fee that includes accommodations and meals.

Another organization, Cotorco, operates a program on the Osa Peninsula at Playa Carate. From August to November, the group constructs a hatchery to protect 100 sea turtle nests. Nests left in place are protected with wire mesh. The specific threats to nests on this beach include predation by dogs, which eat eggs and hatchlings and have even been seen attacking nesting females; poaching; and high tides, which can inundate nests. Primarily olive ridleys and greens nest here, with occasional leatherback and hawksbill nests.

Cotorco welcomes volunteers to help keep the beaches clean and the hatchery running, thereby protecting turtles from poachers and predators. Upon arrival, volunteers receive training by an experienced staff member and have the opportunity to learn about the biology of sea turtles from an on-site biologist. You can volunteer for a minimum of one week, but two are preferable given the need for training. Volunteers work with experienced staff members who are able to demonstrate the proper scientific methods for the work. Responsibilities also include beach patrols, hatchling releases, nest excavations, participation in community projects, speaking with guests, and assisting with turtle data collection and management.

Volunteers can travel to Osa from San José by bus, car, or plane. Lodging options are available for both projects a short walk from the beach. The volunteer program fee covers kayaking and a horseback tour and helps fund the program. As a volunteer, you will have one day off each week to relax and enjoy the beauty of Osa Peninsula.

More information:
Corcovado National Park: 506-735-5036 (international call), costarica-nationalparks.com/corcovadonationalpark.html
Osa Conservation: 202-234-2356, osaconservation.org, seaturtles@osaconservation.org
Cotorco: cotorco.org (in Spanish)

Las Baulas National Park

This park in the heart of the Guanacaste province hosts the highest nesting density of leatherbacks in the eastern Pacific, despite a 95 percent decline in their numbers, which scientists attribute to poaching and the impact of fisheries. The Leatherback Trust operates a research, education, and conservation program here, and volunteers can help with their work to save this critically endangered species.

A nine-day volunteer program run by Earthwatch, housed in the Goldring-Gund Marine Biology Station, focuses on leatherback nesting on Playa Grande and Playa Ventanas. Volunteers participate in nightly beach patrols and, when a nesting female is encountered, help measure and tag her as well as count the eggs and record the nest location. Depending on the season, volunteers may help relocate nests to a hatchery, safeguard the eggs, escort hatchlings to the ocean, record data on nests, or release hatchlings.

Volunteers stay at the Biology Station's cabins on the beach, rooms of four bunk beds split by gender, with bathrooms and air-conditioning. Meals are traditional Costa Rican food eaten at a restaurant just down the beach road, although volunteers prepare their own lunch. Free time can be spent swimming, relaxing on the white-sand beach, exploring tidal pools, touring a mangrove estuary, taking a sailboat cruise, or napping to the sound of howler monkeys in the tropical forest.

More information:
Earthwatch: 800-776-0188, earthwatch.org/exped/paladino.html
Leatherback Trust: 260-481-6305, leatherback.org
Goldring-Gund Marine Biology Station: goldringmarinestation.org/
    Goldring-Gund/Home.html

How to help:
Donate to the Leatherback Trust, or purchase T-shirts, coffee mugs, and other items from the organization.

Las Tortugas Research Station

If you can volunteer from March to June, SEEtheWILD offers trips to Las Tortugas Research Station south of Tortuguero National Park, an area accessible only by boat. Accommodations are basic—just above camping—and there is limited solar power and no hot water. But incredible rain forest landscape surrounds you, and you may wake to the roar of howler monkeys in the jungle. You will also have the chance to make a real difference in conservation of leatherback sea turtles. Spend four hours each evening walking the white-sand beach searching for nesting turtles and, when you find them, help researchers collect data on the mother and move the eggs to a hatchery for safekeeping. Later in the season, from mid-May through June, you will see and work with adorable hatchlings.

On these trips, inevitably someone asks, "How many turtles will we see?" That can be hard to predict, but so far, the turtles have not disappointed, and every year seems better than the one before. Groups almost always encounter leatherbacks within a day or two. The record is within 15 minutes of beginning a patrol. During one educational presentation by a biologist, everyone saw a hatchling up close; the crew had found it on the beach in the early morning and held it until nightfall, when it would have a better chance of safely making it into the ocean. Several participants on one trip even helped dig the nest for a turtle with a missing rear flipper, likely the casualty of an encounter with a shark.

During the day, use free time to explore the rain forest while looking for sloths, monkeys, caimans, and a variety of birds. Visit the Las Tortugas Turtle Museum, help around the hatchery, walk on the beach, or relax in a hammock. Kayaking, ziplining, and soaking in hot springs are other options. Trip extensions to visit Cahuita National Park and Bri Bri Indigenous Reserve in the mountains are also offered.

SEEtheWILD, founded in 2008 as SEE Turtles, has generated hundreds of thousands of dollars for turtle conservation and educated millions of people about the concept of conservation travel. When you take a SEEtheWILD trip, you help provide a source of alternative income for local communities, eliminating the need for poaching and generating support for conservation efforts. The organization partners with tour operators with proven, high-quality service that also support local cultures and economies. This trip partners with EcoTeach, leaders in conservation travel in Costa Rica for nearly 20 years, which places an emphasis on the culture and natural wonders of the country.

More information:
SEEtheWILD: 800-850-4204, seethewild.org
EcoTeach: ecoteach.com

How to help:
Support local businesses, from lodging to restaurants and guides. By doing so, you are helping to make sea turtles a valuable tourism asset and improving the quality of life in surrounding communities.

Osa In-Water Project

WIDECAST manages a conservation project for foraging sea turtles in Playa Blanca on the Osa Peninsula where the Dulce Gulf, one of four tropical fjords worldwide, contains up to 5 percent of global biodiversity. This community-based project started in 2010 with in-water monitoring of eastern Pacific green and hawksbill sea turtles. Today, volunteers participate hands-on with monitoring in the Dulce Gulf, field rescue and rehabilitation, mangrove reforestation, and seagrass monitoring.

Local host families provide accommodation, food, and free-time activities for volunteers. Because this is a foraging area for the sea turtles, volunteers work year-round—a different experience from that on nesting beaches—catching turtles in the water and learning about their behavior and the marine environment. As a volunteer, you will receive training and manuals to learn how to help treat parasites on hawksbills, rehabilitate green and olive ridleys, and help learn more about genetics and blood composition. Volunteers also learn about mangroves and seagrasses, critical habitats for sea turtles and much other marine life and important to humans as well.

Free-time activities include Corcovado National Park tours, snorkel tours, artisanal fishing, bird-watching, kayaking, or just enjoying the lush surroundings with friendly local people.

More information:
WIDECAST Costa Rica: 506-2236-0947 (international call), volunteers@latinamericanseaturtles.org, latinamericanseaturtles.org

How to help:
Adopt a sea turtle at latinamericanseaturtles.org/adoption_program _cr.php, or provide something on the organization's wish list at latinamericanseaturtles.org/wishlist.php.

Ostional Wildlife Refuge

This refuge includes more than 9 miles of Pacific shoreline, on Ostional, Nosara, and Guiones beaches. Olive ridleys nest August through November, with solitary turtles arriving most nights at Ostional, and mass *arribadas* about once a month. The largest *arribadas*, including more than 70,000 individuals, typically occur between August and November. The largest recorded in the past seven years involved an estimated 500,000 sea turtles. An *arribada* is a mass nesting event when thousands or hundreds of thousands of sea turtles congregate offshore, then come onto the beach en masse to nest. These usually happen on dark nights near the quarter moon during rainy season. Scientists are not sure of the purpose of *arribadas*, but one hypothesis is that the sheer numbers of eggs and, later, hatchlings overwhelm predators and ensure that some of the hatchlings survive. This may also be the reason for mass coral spawning and other similar events in nature.

Visitors are allowed on the beach anytime except during an *arribada*, when they must be with a guide, who is available through the Biomarine Station. The Ostional Wildlife Refuge accepts volunteers year-round to help patrol the beach and protect nesting turtles and hatchlings, assist in recording data, or help maintain the park and beach. A daily fee covers food and lodging at a local home or the refuge research station. A two-week minimum stay is requested.

Working Abroad runs a volunteer program in this area as well. This project, operating since 2004, targets long-term monitoring of nesting females and nests to provide data that can be used to formulate management strategies that can be put into practice at this beach. Volunteers can work for less than two weeks or up to three months from December through March. You will take part in nightly beach patrols, collect data from nesting turtles, relocate nests, monitor nests, care for the hatchery, collect hatchling data, and release hatchlings. Room and board are provided in the homes of members of the community. When off-duty, volunteers often relax at the Research Station, which has Wi-Fi service (bring your own computer). The weekly fee covers a private or shared (with another volunteer) room in a homestay, three meals a day, non-alcoholic beverages and snacks, equipment (for patrols), guide during the volunteering, and backup and support.

More information:
Ostional Wildlife Refuge: 501-2682-0400 (international call)
Ostional Guide Association: 506-2682-0428 (international call),
     facebook.com/refugio.ostional?fref=ts
Costa Rica National Parks: costarica-nationalparks.com/
     ostionalwildliferefuge.html or costarica.com/attractions/
     ostional-national-wildlife-refuge/

Arribada Biomarine Station at Ostional: facebook.com/
arribadasostional.costarica
Working Abroad: workingabroad.com/projects/leatherback-and-black-
turtle-project-costa-rica, victoria.mcneil@workingabroad.com

Pacific Sea Turtle Program, Drake Bay

This project in Drake Bay on the northern side of the Osa Peninsula protects primarily olive ridley nests, although some green, leatherback, and hawksbill nests have been recorded here as well. Between 150 and 250 olives nest on the 2-mile-long Drake Beach between the mouth of the River Drake and Punta Ganadito.

Volunteers are needed from July to December for 2 to 12 weeks to perform night surveys on the beach to find nesting turtles and help protect them from poachers and predators, relocate nests to the hatchery, monitor eggs and baby turtles, tag and collect data on nesting turtles, release hatchlings, excavate nests posthatching, maintain the hatchery and camp, and conduct educational activities. Two types of accommodations are available in the village of El Progreso: private rooms in homestay houses or a shared dormitory at the main camp. Both include three meals per day plus snacks for night patrols. At camp, volunteers rotate duties, including cooking, cleaning, and preparing patrol equipment. The main camp includes a communal space equipped with hammocks for relaxing during time off.

A free day every week can be spent on a guided tour of nearby Corcovado National Park, the Isla de Caño Marine Reserve, or other local sights or just resting at the camp. Program personnel help organize tours and other activities as time and resources permit and strive to offer ethical ecotours and excursions that benefit the local community. The weekly fee covers three meals a day, accommodation, snacks for patrols, equipment (for patrols), and guidance.

More information:
Working Abroad: workingabroad.com/projects/pacific-sea-turtle-
programme-costa-rica, victoria.mcneil@workingabroad.com

The Ostional Harvest: Costa Rica Controversy

THE GOVERNMENT of Costa Rica allows the community to harvest eggs at the Ostional Wildlife Refuge on the first day of *arribadas*. Locals collect and sell the eggs, which can be found in San José fish markets and bars. (As noted earlier, some people believe sea turtle eggs are aphrodisiacs, although no scientific evidence supports this.) Local officials say the town takes only 1 percent of the eggs from the beach, but there is no reliable documentation. A study by researchers from the University of Costa Rica reports that 2 percent of the eggs are collected but notes that this is only an estimate. Critics of the harvest say the community takes and sells as many eggs as they can.

When the government authorized the harvest in the early 1980s, few families lived here and the idea was that a legal harvest would reduce poaching. The number of people in the community has since increased dramatically, while individuals still harvest about the same number of eggs, resulting in an increase in the total number of eggs harvested. The scientific jury is still out on the actual number of eggs collected, the number of turtles nesting, and the harvest's effect on turtle reproduction. At least one analysis, however, found no impact of the egg harvest on the ridley population, but scientists noted that this does not prove that there is not one.

Additional studies are under way, and existing data do show that a square meter of beach from which eggs have been harvested produces fewer hatchlings than one on an undisturbed beach. Participants, who understandably defend the harvest, say that many nests in an *arribada* are wasted, as early nests are dug up by turtles nesting later, and that collectors are helping to keep the beach clean. Nature seldom wastes anything, however, nor usually needs our help. Research elsewhere has shown that excess eggs in an *arribada* support the ecosystem by providing nutrients for plants, insects, birds, reptiles, and mammals. The eggs in nests destroyed by subsequent nesting turtles may also serve to satisfy some predators, affording protection to the more recently laid ones. The harvest does remove energy and organic matter from the local ecosystem.

In addition, poaching occurs on nesting beaches elsewhere in Costa Rica that are not actively protected in national parks or wildlife refuges. The fact that eggs from Ostional can legally be sold in markets makes it easy for poachers to sell their product as well; it is impossible to tell whether eggs for sale came from a legal source or an illegal one. Scientists and conservationists working in the country say that the Ostional harvest is used to justify the poaching of eggs elsewhere. Others note that poaching activity happened well before authorization of the harvest, and ending it will not affect poaching and could harm the village. Better monitoring and enforcement against poaching would help, as would efforts to create documentation of the source of legal eggs—and a crackdown on illegal ones. Even a public education campaign to refute the egg's supposed powers—similar to one conducted in Baja California, Mexico—could help.

Since sea turtles are classified as threatened or endangered, and the threats to their existence show no signs of disappearing, the sea turtle conservation community likely will continue to work to change the harvest practice. The community could benefit from increased conservation-based tourism. Currently, residents view the harvest and tourism as inseparable, but many other locations have successful sea turtle tourism without harvests. There is sound evidence that nonconsumptive use of wildlife, such as sea turtle walks, produces three times more economic benefit overall than consumptive use, such as sale of eggs. This issue, and many others involving endangered animals and human interests, is not likely to be solved anytime soon nor to the satisfaction of everyone involved, including the turtles. ∎

More information:

Watch *Between the Harvest*, a film by Scott Drucker: betweentheharvest.com

Read *Saving Sea Turtles: Extraordinary Stories from the Battle against Extinction*, by James Spotila, especially chapter 11, "Ostional: The Egg-Stained Sands of Costa Rica," which documents his travels there

Read "Money Talks: Economic Aspects of Marine Turtle Use and Conservation," by S. Troëng and C. Drews, WWF-International, Gland, Switzerland, wwf.panda.org/about_our_earth/all_publications/?153802/wwwpandaorglacmarineturtlespublications

Read a response from the Costa Rican government: costarica-embassy.org/?q=node/106

How to help:

Support conservation tourism in Ostional. Do not buy sea turtle eggs, even from legal sources, as this creates a market for illegal sources as well.

How to help:

Spend your money on local accommodations, dining, and other activities. This type of income is a sustainable alternative for locals, replacing the collection and sale of turtle eggs or meat.

Pacuare Beach

On remote Pacuare Beach, a 30-mile stretch of black-sand beach accessible only by boat between Tortuguero National Park and the city of Limón, leatherback, green, and occasionally hawksbill sea turtles come to nest. A WIDECAST project here trained former poachers to operate a sea turtle hatchery and rescue center. The organization strives to increase alternative means of support for people in communities in the area, helping to reduce incentives for poaching and ultimately provide long-lasting protection for sea turtles. In addition to the work with sea turtles, the project also teaches people other new skills. For example, a handicraft workshop taught participants how to make jewelry from cow bone and horn rather than hawksbill turtle shell. The jewelry is sold to tourists and volunteers. After one local youngster visited the sea turtle project, his parents stopped selling cream made from turtle oil in their pharmacy. This type of education and information has raised awareness in a region where poaching and illegal hunting still continue.

From March through October, volunteers help patrol the nesting beach, collect data, care for turtles at the rescue center, and escort hatchlings to the water. The volunteer fees provide a vital source of income for local inhabitants. During free time, volunteers can enjoy the beach, relax in a hammock, kayak the lagoons, hike the rain forest, and watch the abundant wildlife, which includes birds, monkeys, coati, and freshwater dolphins.

More information:
To volunteer: latinamericanseaturtles.org

How to help:

Adopt a hatchling at latinamericanseaturtles.org/adoption_program_cr.php, or donate money or items to the project at widecast.org/Support/Donate.html or latinamericanseaturtles.org/wishlist.php.

Parismina

Leatherback and green sea turtles come to beaches on the Caribbean coast of Costa Rica near the mouth of the Parismina River to lay their eggs. Barra de Parismina, a small community just south of Tortuguero National Park, long depended on fishing for turtles and was a hotbed of poaching. In fact, the sea turtle conservation program in the national park actually increased poaching in Parismina. In the late 1990s, a new road and bigger and faster boats only made it easier for poachers to take their products to markets. At one point, 98 percent of the eggs laid on beaches here were poached—until Save the Turtles of Parismina (ASTOP in Spanish) formed in 2001.

With the help of the coast guard, a group of young adults built a hatchery and learned how to relocate and camouflage nests, as well as to measure and tag nesting turtles. They patrolled the beaches every night for no pay. In 2002, a US-based ecotourism company called EcoTeach sent a group to Parismina, and for the first time, the local patrollers were paid. Today ASTOP, a successful, community-based conservation project, involves locals in patrolling, educating children, hosting visitors, and carrying out research. More than 20 locals work as guides, increasing the village income tremendously; other villagers sell crafts, house volunteers, or work in restaurants and shops frequented by visitors. Poaching has dropped to less than 40 percent. Many former poachers even became beach patrollers.

From March to September, patrols cover roughly 4 miles of beach nightly, collecting eggs and taking them to a protected hatchery. ASTOP has released thousands of leatherback hatchlings to date. Data collected on every turtle include time and location of nesting, which helps identify preferred nesting locations and times, making patrolling more effective and helping determine how many turtles are hit by boats or caught in nets.

Volunteers are essential to the success of the Parismina project. They assist with nightly beach patrols, which discourages poaching, and help transfer eggs to the hatchery, monitor the hatchery, and clean the beach of debris, which can interfere with nesting and hatching. Visitors provide most of the project's financial support. Individuals and groups are welcome from March through September or October. Inexpensive lodging options include homestays, hotels, cabins, or camping, running from $10 for a campsite or cabin to $30 for a comfortable room shared with three others, meals included. Although there are several restaurants and small stores, this off-the-grid paradise has no banks, post office, or vehicles, and only one computer with unreliable Internet access. A commitment of a week or two is best, but even those who have only a few days can volunteer.

More information:
Parismina: 506-2798-2220 (international call), parisminaturtles.org, info@parisminaturtles.org

How to help:
If you cannot visit, you can donate to ASTOP or provide something on its wish list. Avoid purchasing any products made from sea turtles.

Other things to do in the area:
Tortuguero National Park. This is the fourth-most-visited national park in Costa Rica. There are a few hiking trails, but a more popular activity is canoeing or kayaking in the natural and human-made canals. Take a guided boat tour of the rain forest and canals to see birds—including the endangered great green macaw—and other wildlife, such as manatees.

Playa Corozalito

On a 5-mile-long beach flanked by a mangrove forest and several rocky outcroppings, Programa Restauración de Tortugas Marinas (PRETOMA), a marine conservation and research NGO founded in 1997, runs a sea turtle conservation project begun here in 2008.

From July 15 to December 15, volunteers patrol the beach nightly for nesting green, olive ridley, and hawksbill sea turtles. Accommodations are in the project station house or private cabins in the town of Corozalito, less than 2 miles away, with meals prepared by a cook. The town also has a soccer pitch, site of many a friendly pickup match, and off time can be spent hiking in the forest, horseback riding, swimming, surfing, and exploring the beach in daylight.

More information:
PRETOMA: 506-2241-5227 (international call), turtle-trax.com/
   beach-projects/corozalito/

How to help:
   Donate to support PRETOMA's research, outreach, education, conservation, and advocacy efforts.

Punta Islita

   Located on the Nicoya Peninsula near the town of Islita, just about 3
miles from Corozalito, this luxury resort of 47 casitas overlooks the Pacific.
A reforestation project has planted thousands of trees, and the resort
composts organic waste and recycles its trash. The pools are solar heated,
and much of the food served is organic. From June to November, three
nights a week, guests can visit Camaronal Beach nearby to observe nesting turtles. The hotel works in cooperation with the Camaronal Foundation and Costa Rican Ministry of Environment.

More information:
Punta Islita: 866-446-4053, hotelpuntaislita.com

Tortuguero National Park

   No other organization has been studying and protecting sea turtles
longer than the Sea Turtle Conservancy (STC), founded more than 50
years ago by Archie Carr as the Caribbean Conservation Corporation.
Few have achieved more success in recovering sea turtle populations.
The Smithsonian Natural History Museum recognized STC's long-term
green turtle recovery program at Tortuguero, Costa Rica, as one of the
world's greatest marine conservation success stories. STC has worked
with the community of Tortuguero since 1959 to protect green turtles on
one of the most important nesting beaches in the world, producing a 500
percent increase in the nesting population. Today, the Tortuguero green
turtle colony is by far the largest in the Western Hemisphere.

STC offers eco-volunteer adventures here March through November, for one, two, or three weeks. As a volunteer, you work March to June with leatherback turtles and June through November with greens. Volunteers participate in nightly sea turtle walks on the black-sand beach, covering 5 to 6 miles in four or five hours, helping to find, tag, and record data on turtles and to count tracks to help determine nesting activity in particular areas. Your presence also serves as a powerful deterrent to poachers.

For accommodations, choose between rustic, dorm-style housing in the rain forest with bunk beds and community baths or private rooms in the scientists' residence for an additional fee. Three meals a day and snacks, featuring authentic Costa Rican dishes, are included. You will have leisure time for exploring the park, which includes jungle trails and a series of natural canals presenting incredible opportunities for viewing wildlife. Visits to the nearby village of Tortuguero and talking with research biologists are other options.

More information:
Sea Turtle Conservancy: 352-373-6441, conserveturtles.org

How to help:
Your visit helps support the science station and its research. You can also become a member of or make a donation to STC, supporting its work in the United States and wider Caribbean. Or you can adopt a turtle for yourself or as a gift for someone else.

Other things to do in the area:
Cahuita National Park. The park offers tremendous bird and wildlife watching; you may see howler and white-faced monkeys, two- and three-toed sloths, toucans, iguanas, butterflies, or frogs. Guided nature tours are recommended. The park has hiking trails, and area tour operators offer hiking tours.

Scuba diving and snorkeling. These are popular activities over the area's coral reefs. There are more than 20 dive sites between Cahuita and Manzanillo, home to Costa Rica's only two living coral reefs, as well as two shipwrecks. Best visibility for snorkeling is February to April, and equipment can be rented from hotels and beachfront kiosks. For attractions in the park, see costarica.com/attractions/cahuita-national-park/.

✄ *El Salvador*

In the indigenous language, the name of this country, Custcatlan, means "land of jewels." Those jewels include more than 300 rivers, volcanic lakes, mountain ranges, and Pacific coast beaches popular with surfers and frequented by hawksbill, green, and olive ridley sea turtles.

A ministry of environment and natural resources was established only in the late 1990s, so this smallest Central American country is officially a relative newcomer to conservation. The government banned the consumption, sale, and possession of sea turtles, their eggs, and their parts for purposes other than conservation (this leaves Guatemala as the only country to allow unrestricted egg collection).

Before the ban, an estimated 4,000 El Salvadorans collected the eggs to sell in markets of major cities like La Libertad and San Salvador, as well as in small towns along the coast. That left few nests untouched. While these *tortugueros*, as they are called in the country, do not completely depend on this money for survival, this revenue can be significant. So, instead of making nesting beaches into protected areas and closing them to local residents, El Salvador created a network of hatcheries and pays *tortugueros* for bringing in the eggs that they find. At the hatcheries, the eggs are put into artificial nests and protected until they hatch and the hatchlings are released into the ocean.

In 2009, the government, with support from the US Agency for International Development (USAID) and several conservation organizations, expanded the hatchery system across the coast. *Tortugueros* are paid $2.50 for every 14 eggs, so with an olive ridley nest averaging 110 eggs, they can earn about $20 from a single nest. While many conservationists here believe that collecting eggs is a purely economic activity, others see a strong social element to the activity. *Tortugueros* use the words *pastime*, *sport*, and *habit* to describe egg collecting and talk about building bonds with the other men.

The expanded payment program had a dramatic effect on the protection of turtle eggs. In 2008, the year before the ban was established, roughly 180,000 eggs were saved. In 2009, that number jumped to 1 million, and it grew to 1.5 million in 2010 and 2011, about 80 percent of all of the turtle eggs laid in the country. This stunning increase is primarily the result of the infusion of funds from USAID, however, and not the law itself.

Bahia Jiquilisco Biosphere Preserve

Bahia Jiquilisco on the southeastern Pacific coast of El Salvador is home to an Eastern Pacific Hawksbill Initiative (ICAPO) project that offers both volunteer and group travel opportunities. El Salvador's largest wetland, blue water ringed by volcanoes looming over the water like giant sentries, is critical habitat for wildlife and fisheries.

Named a UNESCO Biosphere Preserve in 2007, Bahia Jiquilisco contains 245 square miles of some of the most untouched natural landscape in the Americas, home to a variety of birds and about 40 percent of nesting hawksbills in the eastern Pacific. Since 2008, the ICAPO team has patrolled beaches, tagged and gathered data on turtles, and taken eggs to one of two protected hatcheries. On one beach, nests are protected in place. Local residents known as *careyeros* (from the Spanish name for hawksbill, *carey*) help collect eggs here, just as they do in Padre Ramos. As of the 2012 season, the project protected more than 300 nests, released 33,500 hatchlings, and benefited 95 local families.

A volunteer program provides a sustainable source of income for the project and makes an important contribution to the labor-intensive conservation efforts. Volunteer stints run one to four weeks and include accommodations, three meals a day prepared by community staff, and training. SEEtheWILD, in partnership with EcoViva, an organization that promotes community development and natural resource protection, recently organized volunteer service trips based on the small island of La Pirraya, accessible only by boat. An annual Hawksbill Turtle Festival has become the area's major social event of the year, a combination of parades, traditional dancing, speakers, a clown, and other festivities. It serves as an important way to educate local residents about the importance of protecting sea turtles.

While the discovery and protection of these two nesting sites gives new hope for the future of hawksbill turtles in the region, it also creates a sense of urgency to address threats facing them. A serious threat comes from blast fishing, a method that uses a mixture of sugar, chlorate, and sulfur to create an explosion, killing anything within an estimated radius of up to 80 feet, including turtles. ICAPO estimates that more than 25 hawksbills have been killed by blast fishing in Jiquilisco Bay since 2004—out of a total estimated regional population of fewer than 1,000 turtles. The organization recently formed a partnership with EcoViva to address this practice and lobby the government to enforce laws against this illegal fishing practice.

In a few short years, this small group of scientists and local residents has managed to upend the scientific consensus regarding both where hawksbill turtles live and their status in this region. Groundbreaking scientific research, the protection of 90 percent of hawksbill eggs laid in both sites, and 200 local residents working to protect hawksbills on a budget equivalent to what some large nonprofits spend on membership mailings alone are just a few of the highlights.

More information:
ICAPO program: hawksbill.org/volunteer.html, volunteers@hawksbill.org
SEEtheWILD Conservation Tours: seethewild.org
EcoViva Community Empowerment Tours: http://eco-viva.org/tours/
    community-empowerment-tours.html

How to help:
Participate in the ICAPO volunteer program, join a conservation tour to El Salvador with EcoViva, or donate through the Save the Hawksbills Fund.

Guatemala

More than half of the population of this country claims indigenous heritage, mostly Mayan. Many still dress in traditional style and live in homes with thatched roofs. The inland region remains heavily forested, and coastal mangrove forests are relatively intact.

In 1989, a group of Guatemalan citizens concerned about the disappearance of their natural heritage, especially their wildlife, founded Asociación de Rescate y Conservación de Vida Silvestre (ARCAS), an NGO committed to preserving wildlife and habitat. The organization's first and still its largest project is a wildlife rescue center in the northern Petén region of the country. One of the largest and most complex rescue centers in the world, it handles 300 to 600 confiscated animals representing more than 40 species.

Akazul

Akazul was formed in 2010 by a group from Project Parlama, which was developed by Ambios (a UK-based nonprofit) and ARCAS to standardize and strengthen Guatemala's sea turtle conservation efforts by connecting sea turtle hatcheries along the coast, conducting valuable research, and providing environmental education activities within these communities. Akazul continues to work on a grassroots level with coastal communities and other Guatemalan NGOs, encouraging local participation in natural resource management to ensure healthy and productive ecosystems in the future.

The name comes from an ancient Mayan myth; Ak was the "great cosmic turtle," the constellation known today as Orion. What is now Orion's belt represented a crack in the cosmic turtle's shell, from where Hero Twins emerged to create life on earth. *Azul*, the Spanish word for "blue," represents the ocean.

The project is based in the small coastal village of La Barrona, Jutiapa, on the Guatemalan Pacific coast a few miles west of the El Salvador border. These 5 miles of black volcanic-sand beach are important nesting ground for olive ridleys and leatherbacks.

Akazul uses volunteers for conducting nightly beach patrols (minimum four hours per night), helping collect scientific data and monitor nesting sea turtles, managing hatcheries (including egg burial, hatchling release, and posthatching nest excavations), monitoring habitat, surveying local flora and fauna, and helping with various community-based conservation activities, including environmental education classes, capacity-building workshops, and social surveys.

Volunteers are asked to make a minimum time commitment of four weeks (but shorter terms will be considered) and stay with local families, who provide a basic, comfortable room and three meals a day. Volunteers need to make their own travel and insurance arrangements and support themselves financially throughout their stay. The experience is greatly enhanced by having a basic understanding of the Spanish language, and many good schools offer Spanish-language courses in Guatemala, including in and around Antigua, Xela, and Lago de Atitlán.

More information:
Akazul: akazul.org

How to help:
Become a member, sponsor a nest, or donate.

Parque Hawaii

On the Pacific coast, just east of Monterrico, Parque Hawaii is home to a sea turtle and mangrove conservation project run by ARCAS. Its original purpose was to build a rescue center to care for and rehabilitate wild animals confiscated on the black market. It continues to do this, along with public and environmental education and sea turtle, mangrove, and community development projects on the Pacific coast.

In Parque Hawaii, the project manages two hatcheries, collecting up to 40,000 olive ridley, green, and leatherback eggs for safe hatching each year. During nesting season, volunteers walk the beach each night in search of nesting turtles, helping to collect eggs and move them to the hatcheries. When eggs begin hatching, volunteers excavate nests and help with releases, held at night or early or late in the day to protect hatchlings from the heat and predators. Volunteers also help record data concerning nests, hatching rates, and other research efforts.

Olive ridley nesting season runs June to October, and leatherbacks nest in November and December (although, sadly, their numbers are drastically declining in the Pacific). Turtle eggs continue to serve as food for local populations, and most turtle eggs are collected and sold. The take and sale of sea turtle eggs are legal as long as individuals contribute at least 20 percent of eggs collected to one of the ARCAS hatcheries. Volunteers help take in these donated eggs and bury them in the hatchery.

There is volunteer work to be done year-round, including environmental education, mangrove monitoring, and research. Volunteers can combine this unique experience saving the sea turtles of the Pacific coast of Guatemala with working at ARCAS's wildlife rescue center in the northern Petén region of the country near the world-renowned Mayan ruins of Tikal.

Volunteers pay their own travel expenses, cover any special needs such as a restricted diet, and pay a per-week fee that helps support the work of ARCAS and covers accommodation in volunteer houses with electricity, full kitchen, and bathrooms. There is access to hammocks and a lookout tower on the beach. Volunteers can prepare their own meals or dine with local families for a small fee (about $2.50 per meal). Homestays with area families are another option.

More information:
ARCAS: 502-7830-1374 (international call), arcasguatemala.com

How to help:
In addition to volunteering at ARCAS, you can donate items listed on the organization's wish list.

Nicaragua

This lesser-known and still relatively unspoiled Central American country has beautiful beaches, seven types of forests, volcanoes, colonial cities, and two large inland bodies of water, Lake Nicaragua and Lake Managua. All of this adds up to an incredible amount of biodiversity. Cloud forests shelter exotic birds such as quetzals and green macaws, and humpback whales swim offshore. Four species of sea turtle are found in the waters of Nicaragua's Caribbean and Pacific coasts—hawksbills, greens, leatherbacks, and olive ridleys. It is also home to two important sea turtle nesting beaches, Padre Ramos Estuary and La Flor Wildlife Refuge.

Nicaragua makes admirable efforts to protect its incredible landscape and wildlife, but poverty, population growth, and climate change are formidable challenges to those efforts. The fishing industry here accidentally catches thousands of sea turtles every year, and poaching for eggs and shell continues to be a serious threat. Conservation and tourism programs offer a sustainable alternative to fishing and poaching and will help protect habitat from unsustainable development.

Estero Padre Ramos Nature Reserve

Declared a protected area in 1983, this reserve on the northwestern coast of Nicaragua includes beaches that host roughly 45 percent of all hawksbill nesting activity in the entire eastern Pacific. Not long ago, many sea turtle experts assumed there were too few hawksbills along the Pacific coast of the Americas to bother protecting. But this opinion assumed that hawksbills in the region would live almost exclusively around coral reefs, as they do just about everywhere else in the world. This coast has relatively few reefs, so scientists believed there must be fewer turtles. In addition, no beaches along this coast had been identified as major hawksbill nesting sites, making it even more difficult to estimate population size.

Then, in 2008, Alexander Gaos and his wife, Ingrid Yanez, began researching hawksbills in Baja California, Mexico, and talking to other turtle conservationists in the region. They met Michael Liles, a turtle researcher and now director of the Eastern Pacific Hawksbill Initiative,

A female hawksbill in Nicaragua. (Photo by Brad Nahill/SEEtheWILD)

known by its Spanish acronym, ICAPO, in El Salvador. ICAPO collaborates with local communities, scientists, and policy makers in the region and has established many conservation projects. Liles had recently discovered hawksbills nesting in Jiquilisco Bay in that country. The three organized a meeting in El Salvador and invited turtle conservationists from around the region, determined to find other nesting sites. One attendee, José Urteaga, Nicaragua coordinator at Fauna & Flora International (FFI), reported another potential nesting site in northwestern Nicaragua. We now know that two nesting areas, less than 100 miles apart and unknown to science just a few years ago, account for roughly 90 percent of known hawksbill nesting on the Pacific coast between Mexico and Ecuador.

FFI works here in partnership with ICAPO and the Hawksbill Committee, 18 local nonprofit organizations, community groups, local governments, and others. Since 2010, a local research team has patrolled the beaches every night during the season, April 15 to September 15, tagging and recording data on turtles, protecting them from poachers, and bringing eggs into a hatchery for safe incubation. On one island in the reserve, the team leaves nests in place but monitors and protects them. In its first year, the project protected 300 nests, released more than 25,000 hatchlings, and benefited 80 local families.

Volunteers provide essential support, both physical and monetary, for the project and the community. They work eight hours per day, on beach patrols, egg collection, management of the hatchery, boat patrols of the estuary, community interaction, and general maintenance of facilities. It can be strenuous, but participants consider the opportunity to make a difference, meet new people, and contribute to research and conservation ample reward. Individuals can join for one week up to five months, although a minimum stay of two weeks is recommended. A program fee covers orientation, three meals a day provided by community staff, accommodations, and training. Volunteers pay their own airfare into Managua, 115 miles away, and have several affordable options for travel to the reserve.

Tourism has barely touched Padre Ramos, and conservation takes many forms. The primary way these turtles are protected is by enlisting the help of *careyeros* to bring eggs from nests around the estuary to the hatcheries. The *careyeros* know these turtles better than anyone else but, before this project was founded in 2010, sold most of the eggs they collected on the black market. Now, both here and in El Salvador, *careyeros* are paid by conservation groups for their work, earning income for the number of eggs they bring, as well as how many hatch, which encourages careful handling of the eggs.

More information:
ICAPO: hawksbill.org/volunteer.html, volunteers@hawksbill.org
Fauna & Flora International: fauna-flora.org/explore/nicaragua/

How to help:
Avoid imported farmed shrimp; shrimp farms in Nicaragua threaten the health of Padre Ramos Estuary.

La Flor Wildlife Refuge

San Juan Del Sur, a mecca for surfers, beachgoers, and retirees, lies on the southern Pacific coast, a string of idyllic bays surrounded by green rolling hills. Locals here work to preserve sea turtles and the unique tropical dry forest habitat. Paso Pacifico, a conservation organization founded in 2005, partners with local communities to provide alternatives to poaching of sea turtle eggs and deforestation.

Just south of San Juan Del Sur, the Refugio De Vida Silvestre La Flor is an important nesting area primarily for olive ridleys, as well as hawksbills, leatherbacks, and greens. This is one of two nesting areas in Nicaragua where olive ridleys nest in *arribadas*, between July and December. In the 2008 season, more than 180,000 nests were laid on La Flor beaches.

SEEtheWILD offers three trip options. The first is "Nicaragua Wildlife Adventure," in partnership with Wildland Adventures, which includes two days on the nesting beach in La Flor Wildlife Refuge, where you stay on the beach in the village of San Juan del Sur. From July through January, you will take part in guided night beach walks to witness olive ridleys nesting or perhaps a hatchling release. The trips include tours of the colonial city of León, a hike up Cerro Negro volcano, ziplining through the forest at Mombacho volcano, exploring the cafés and museums of Granada, boating on Lake Nicaragua, and a community activity such as a bonfire or farm visit.

Another option, "Cloudforest, Reefs and Sea Turtles," in partnership with the Mesoamerican Ecotourism Alliance, spends two nights in San

Juan del Sur and a full day at La Flor. This itinerary includes several days in mountainous, coffee-producing regions, with excellent bird-watching; hiking through cloud forest searching for orchids and through the Indio Maíz Biological Reserve; visiting museums and artisan shops in San Carlos; and tubing on the Río San Juan.

The "Nicaragua's Wild Side" trip, in partnership with Reefs to Rockies, overnights at Morgan's Rock Ecolodge for a day on La Flor's nesting beaches; other stops on this trip include hiking Montibelli Nature Reserve to see exotic birds, such as hundreds of green parakeets, and a waterfall; a visit to Los Guatuzus Wildlife Reserve and a boat ride on the Río San Juan; stops in the Indio Maíz Biological Reserve to see birds, monkeys, sloths, poison dart frogs, and wildcats; exploring colonial Granada; and a night hike up Mombacho volcano.

More information:
SEEtheWILD: seethewild.org

How to help:
Donate to Nicaragua sea turtles through Paso Pacifico, a US 501(c)(3) organization: pasopacifico.org/saveseaturtles.html.

Other things to do in the area:
Indio Maíz Biological Reserve. Hike the cloud forest in the reserve as you look for birds, monkeys, wildcats, sloths, and other wildlife.
Bird-watching. Watch for birds in the coffee-producing regions.
Río San Juan. Tube on the river.

Morgan's Rock Hacienda and Ecolodge

This lodge is located on the coast just north of the border between Nicaragua and Costa Rica. Some 70 percent of the food served here is grown on-site using an innovative irrigation system, and the lodge has planted more than 1.5 million tropical trees for sustainable harvest. Monkeys, wild birds, sloths, and other wild animals live in the surrounding jungle, and bungalows line a cliff above a private white-sand beach. Guests can take part in guided tours to watch nesting sea turtles or hatchlings August through February, at no extra charge.

More information:

Morgan's Rock: 505-2563-9005 (international call), morgansrock.com

Pearl Cays Wildlife Refuge

This refuge, a network of 22 remote cays located 2 to 15 miles off the eastern coast of Nicaragua, supports the largest remaining hawksbill rookery in the west-central Caribbean. Its waters are part of Nicaragua's vast system of seagrass, providing forage for the largest aggregation of green sea turtles in the Atlantic. Loggerhead and leatherback turtles also forage in or migrate through the area.

Since 1997, the Wildlife Conservation Society (WCS) has been monitoring sea turtle populations and promoting conservation at the local and national levels. The Pearl Cays Hawksbill Project has decreased poaching of eggs by more than 80 percent and also reduced the killing of nesting females. As with many successful conservation efforts, an integral part of this one is developing appropriate alternative sources of income, such as community-based tourism, for resource users. Coastal indigenous and ethnic fishers still capture green sea turtles and sell the meat for income, and WCS is working with fishers from the Miskitu community of Kahkabila to substitute income earned from turtle fishing with that from ecotourism. A group of them formed Kabu Tours (*Kabu* means "ocean" in the Miskitu language) to offer hawksbill watch tours during the nesting season and reef snorkeling tours year-round. Participants on the hawksbill tours may be able to meet and talk with WCS staff working on nesting data collection.

More information:

Wildlife Conservation Society: wcs.org/saving-wild-places/ocean/pearl-
     cayes-nicaragua.aspx
Kabu Tours: kabutours.com

How to help:

By choosing only community-based tourism providers, you help support the development of alternative sources of income for green turtle fishers.

⛝ *Panama*

A narrow arc between Costa Rica and Colombia, this country has long coastlines on the Caribbean Sea and the Pacific Ocean. Natural features include a mountainous spine, rain forests, many beaches, and numerous islands, although its most famous feature is the human-made Panama Canal.

Four species of sea turtle—loggerhead, leatherback, green, and hawksbill—nest and forage in Bocas del Toro Province. Since 1989, scientists from the Florida Fish and Wildlife Conservation Commission, Florida Marine Research Institute, and Eckerd College in Florida, with support from the Wildlife Conservation Society, have studied sea turtle ecology and migration here. The first legal protections for sea turtles in Panama were adopted in 1967, but current rules and regulations are not always clear. WIDECAST has a long history of working to restore and protect the nesting hawksbill population at Chiriqui Beach in Bocas del Toro.

Guna Yala

On the Caribbean coast of Panama, just north of Colombia, is a region known as Guna Yala, or Land of the Guna, who are an indigenous people. To many, this strip of coast and 365-island archipelago is known as San Blas. It remains relatively unspoiled, with pristine beaches and incredible blue seas.

Locals coordinate a conservation program, Conservación de las Tortugas Marinas, in Armila, the southernmost Guna Yala village near the Colombian border and one of the most important nesting beaches for leatherbacks. Volunteers can help the organization with monitoring, collecting data, and general assistance. Accommodations are available, but volunteers must pay for their own meals.

Eco-resort Ibedi al Natural offers guided turtle walks in the Armila beach sanctuary from February to August. Guests often see nesting leatherbacks and hawksbills—as many as 80 in a single night—or hatchling releases. The eco-resort has spacious aboveground cabins made with local bamboo and wood, featuring twin or double beds, fans, and hammocks. Lush natural landscaping surrounds the cabins and an open-air dining area. Other activities include swimming, snorkeling, Guna cultural tours, boat tours, and fishing.

The first Sea Turtle Festival of Panama took place in Armila in 2010, and the event happens annually during May, which is considered the "moon of turtles" here. Festivalgoers are likely to see nesting leatherbacks at night and in the early morning, and those willing to stay up late and walk farther on the beach may see many nesting turtles and hundreds of hatchlings. Officials from the Guna General Congress, Panamanian environmental agencies, Smithsonian Tropical Research Center, Sea Turtle Conservancy, Panamanian Ministries of Tourism and Industry, and Ocean Revolution attend, along with tourists and members of many neighboring communities. The festival has led to establishment of a scientific research outpost, new collaborations between government agencies and NGOs, and increased scientific and cultural knowledge about these magnificent animals and the benefit to communities themselves.

More information:

Ibedi al Natural and Conservación de las Tortugas Marinas: 507-6563-0554 (international call), ibedialnatural.net/ or yaukgalu.com/ (in Spanish)

Sea Turtle Festival: oceanrevolution.org/projects.html

How to help:

Donate to the organization through yaukgalu.com. Sales of *Gammibe Gun Galu*, an album of local music, support conservation efforts in the region: gammibegungalu.bandcamp.com/.

Green sea turtle. (Photo by Bethany Resnick)

South America

⚑ *Brazil*

T HE LARGEST country in South America, Brazil contains an incredible biodiversity. It also offers almost every experience for travelers, from beaches to rain forests, waterfalls, canyons, and the world's largest wetland, the Pantanal, 20 times the size of the Florida Everglades. Brazil has more than 4,650 miles of coastline on the South Atlantic Ocean.

Five species of sea turtles can be found along that coastline. Their numbers have declined drastically from consumption of meat and eggs, illegal fishing, and beach use, but 23 stations in nine Brazilian states now protect roughly 20,000 nests annually. A Brazilian nonprofit founded in 1980, Projeto TAMAR, for Tartaruga Marinha, the Portuguese word for "sea turtle," monitors more than 620 miles of the country's beaches.

Fernando de Noronha

This 21-island archipelago off the coast of Brazil sits just four degrees south of the equator in incredibly blue ocean. TAMAR began operating here in 1984, when the archipelago was still a federal territory. Due to the organization's efforts, Lion, the main nesting beach for sea turtles, became the seed for a marine park, Fernando de Noronha National Park, created by federal decree in 1988. The park takes in 70 percent of the archipelago and, thanks to incredible volcanic rock formations, tropical plants, and a wealth of indigenous wildlife—including two birds found only here, albatrosses, tortoises, sea turtles, and dolphins—it earned World Heritage Site status in 2001. Tourists come mainly to surf and scuba dive in the warm, clear waters.

TAMAR monitors nesting of green turtles and runs a program to mark juvenile green and hawksbill turtles that forage here. A visitor center, built following environmentally friendly practices, opened in 1996 with the purpose of attracting tourists to local environmental programs, and each year about 45,000 people participate. The visitor center offers

139

SOUTH AMERICA

Fernando de
Noronha

BRAZIL

PACIFIC
OCEAN

URUGUAY
Cerro Verde

ATLANTIC
OCEAN

N
W · E
S

0   250   500   750 miles
0   250   500   750 kilometers

themed programs nightly and diving, hiking, and other tours. It also has exhibits on sea turtles.

Visitors can participate in hatchling releases and can observe night monitoring of the nesting beach in Praia do Leao, which has the highest concentration of nesting in the archipelago, from December to June. Visitors can also observe the capture, marking, and recapture of turtles throughout the year. There are some volunteer opportunities; contact the project for details.

More information:
Projeto TAMAR: tamar.org.br (in Portuguese)

🏴 *Uruguay*

The second-smallest country in South America, wedged between Brazil and Argentina, Uruguay has more than 400 miles of coastline on the South Atlantic Ocean. The country is divided into departments, governmental entities similar to states.

Although Uruguay has no nesting beaches, green, loggerhead, leatherback, and olive ridley sea turtles do forage in the waters off its coast. In 1999, a group of college students, researchers, and biologists formed a nonprofit organization to pursue sea turtle research and conservation. They called the organization Karumbé, which means "turtle" in the language of the Guarani, the first inhabitants of this coast.

Cerro Verde

Located in the coastal department of Rocha, Cerro Verde includes two protected areas—the Bañados del Este and Coastal Fringe Biosphere Reserves—which contain a high diversity of flora and fauna, including dolphins, sea lions, and birds. A broad, V-shaped beach fronts shallow blue sea. The water is cool here on the southern end of the continent. For more than 13 years, Karumbé has had a sea turtle project here, working mainly with juvenile green sea turtles but also with stranded loggerhead, leatherback, and hawksbill turtles. The organization also monitors local artisanal fisheries and collects bycatch data.

Volunteers can participate in all Karumbé's activities. They help with research and conservation activities, including outreach to fishers, capture of sea turtles for data collection, beach walks to search for stranded turtles, assistance with necropsies, educational programs with the community and tourists, and help with turtle rehabilitation. Speaking Spanish is helpful but not required, and volunteers need to be in good physical condition. Training is provided in both English and Spanish. A maximum of 16 volunteers can work at any particular time.

More information:
Karumbé: karumbe.org
To volunteer: karumbealdia.blogspot.com/, facebook.com/karumbe.org,
    volkarumbe@gmail.com

Mediterranean Sea

OGGERHEADS nest mostly in the eastern portion of the Mediterranean, primarily in Cyprus, Greece, and in smaller numbers in Turkey. Small numbers of loggerhead nests have been recorded in Egypt, Israel, Italy, Libya, Syria, and Tunisia. Based on the recorded number of nests per year in Cyprus, Greece, Israel, Tunisia, and Turkey, loggerhead nesting in the Mediterranean ranges from about 3,300 to 7,000 nests per season.

Greens nest on Turkey's Mediterranean coast. Dense human population and related development along these coasts have reduced sea turtle nesting throughout the sea.

Mediterranean Association to Save the Sea Turtles, Athens

The Mediterranean Association to Save the Sea Turtles (MEDASSET) was founded in 1988 to protect sea turtles and their habitats throughout the Mediterranean by carrying out research programs, campaigns, education, and political lobbying. The organization has conducted studies all along the Mediterranean coastline, from the northeastern Aegean and Ionian Seas to the coast of Turkey, Syria, Lebanon, Egypt, Libya, and more recently, Albania. MEDASSET has been a partner to the Mediterranean Action Plan of the United Nations Environmental Programme (UNEP/MAP) and a permanent member/observer of the Bern Convention of the Council of Europe since 1988.

Volunteers are welcome at the MEDASSET office in Athens for periods of three to five weeks. For those who want to help but cannot come in person, the organization offers the opportunity to become "e-volunteers" and help out via the Internet. Unpaid internship opportunities are available for university students and professional adults who are looking for international work experience, to improve their language skills, or

possibly earn academic credit. To apply for one of these spots, complete the application form on the MEDASSET website (click on "Make a Difference" and then "Volunteer" on the home page).

More information:
MEDASSET: 210-3640389 (international call), medasset.org, medasset@ medasset.gr

How to help:
The organization relies on public support to continue its scientific research, environmental education, and awareness-raising programs. Join Friends of MEDASSET, or make a donation online: medasset.org (click

"Support Our Work" on the home page). Order limited-edition and original objects from the MEDASSET gift shop to help support its conservation and education work throughout the Mediterranean.

The Sea Turtle Protection Society of Greece, Zakynthos

Since 1983, the Sea Turtle Protection Society of Greece (ARCHELON), a nonprofit NGO, has protected sea turtles and their habitats in Greece. It monitors turtle populations, manages nesting beaches, provides environmental education and public awareness programs, and rehabilitates injured turtles. The society has monitored main loggerhead nesting areas in Greece—including Zakynthos, Kyparissia Bay, Karoni, Lakonikos Bay, Rethymno Messaras Bay, and Chania Bay. ARCHELON works with state agencies, local authorities, institutions, other NGOs, associations of fishers, and citizens to mitigate threats to and reverse population decline of sea turtles. It relies heavily on volunteers, with more than 400 volunteers from all over the world participating in its work each year.

Nesting season runs from mid-May until mid-August. Volunteers who arrive early in the season, in May or June, help build the campsite in an olive grove and prepare for the coming nesting season. Work at the site includes surveying for adult turtle tracks and nests, relocating threatened nests or placing protective cages around nests, tagging nesting females, and dealing with injured or dead turtles. During hatching season, which starts mid-July and lasts until the end of October, volunteers also help with morning surveys for hatchling tracks, marking of hatching nests, assisting hatchlings that are still on the beach, and excavating hatched nests.

The main threat to sea turtles is coastal development, which destroys nesting beaches and introduces threats such as speedboats. Nesting beaches on Zakynthos are heavily used by tourists, so to protect the nests, beaches, and turtles, the project conducts a public-awareness program. Volunteers help with this as well by informing visitors about sea turtles and the ways visitors can help save them. This work is done from early May until the end of the season and involves talking to beachgoers on beach patrols, guarding nesting beaches at night to prevent people from disturbing turtles, running an information kiosk, and giving slide shows at hotels and on turtle-spotting boats. At the end of the season, volunteers help dismantle the camp and store materials for the following season.

The campsite is basic but comfortable, with cooking facilities, showers, and toilets. ARCHELON constantly works to improve living conditions, but volunteers are responsible for maintaining and running the campsite.

More information:
ARCHELON: +30-210-5231342 (international call), archelon.gr (click on the British flag for English version, and on "Become a volunteer" to apply as a volunteer)

How to help:
Purchase a sea turtle souvenir from ARCHELON's website, adopt a turtle, or make a donation. See "Support" and "How to help" on the home page of the website.

Other things to do in the area:
Water sports. Snorkel or scuba dive in underwater caves. Go sailing or surfing.
Hiking. Hike trails in the mountains.

Africa

HUMANS most likely originated from the continent of Africa, with modern humans arising there more than 200,000 years ago. Sea turtles, of course, have been there much longer. The world's second-largest continent, Africa has coastline on the Mediterranean Sea, Red Sea, eastern Atlantic Ocean, and western Indian Ocean. Green, loggerhead, olive ridley, leatherback, and hawksbill sea turtles are found in waters off the coasts of Africa. Greens nest at several locations on Africa's Atlantic and Indian Ocean coasts; hawksbills, on the Guinea and East African coasts. Solitary olive ridleys nest on the shores of a number of West African countries: South Africa, Mozambique, Kenya, and Tanzania. Cape Verde hosts an important loggerhead nesting population, and loggerheads also nest in South Africa, Mozambique, and Madagascar. Gabon, Mozambique, and South Africa contain leatherback nesting beaches.

Cape Verde

Cape Verde, an island-nation 350 miles off the western coast of Africa, is the third-most-important loggerhead nesting area in the world. Loggerheads nest on the islands of Boavista and Sal; in 2000, researchers tagged more than 1,000 nesting females on just 3.1 miles of Boavista's beaches. These islands were first inhabited by the Portuguese in the 1400s and used as a stop on transoceanic journeys. Portuguese remains the primary language, and the culture retains a vibrant mix of those of Portugal and Africa. Ten major islands—five Barlavento, or windward, and five Sotavento, or leeward—form an eastward-pointing V shape in the warm, clear waters of the Atlantic Ocean.

Olive ridley returning to the sea. (Photo by Guillaume Feuillet)

AFRICA

Cape Verde
- SOS Tartarugas, Sal
- Boa Vista

Ghana
- Winneba
- Ada Foah

- Libreville
- Gamba **Gabon**
- Mayumba

ATLANTIC OCEAN

Kenya
- Malindi Marine Park
- Watamu Marine National Park and Reserve

- Vamizi Island
- Quirimbas National Park

Mozambique
- Bazaruto Archipelago National Park
- Ponta do Ouro Partial Marine Reserve
- iSimangaliso Wetland Park

South Africa

N
W—E
S

0   250   500   750 miles
0   250 500 750 kilometers

Boa Vista

The Turtle Foundation (TF), a nongovernmental organization, was established in 2000 in Germany and has operated conservation projects in Indonesia since 2000 and on the Cape Verdean island of Boa Vista since 2008. The Boa Vista effort began after the organization learned that more than 1,100 turtles were slaughtered coming ashore to nest in 2007. From protecting one beach in 2008, it grew to protecting five by 2010, with support from the local military and international volunteers. The foundation focuses on youth and community education, collaborates with local tour operators on ecotourism, and works to find alternative sources of income for the community. The 2012 season saw higher nesting activity on Boa Vista than in the previous four years—3,618 nests—and fewer dead turtles than in previous years as well.

Tourists on Boa Vista can attend informational talks at the beach camps, and tour operators take groups to visit the camps, where they learn about the negative effects of driving motorized vehicles on nesting beaches (quad tours on beaches are popular on the island, unfortunately), the work of the Turtle Foundation, and sustainable tourism. Turtle-watching tours are conducted in collaboration with three small, local tour operators, and the group plans to expand this activity. The project also plans to begin training local staff as turtle-watching guides as part of its pursuit of high-quality but small-scale tours that meet species protection goals while also benefiting the local population.

Volunteers are needed during the nesting season, June 15 to November 1, from two weeks to five months. Duties range from monitoring nesting beaches to collecting data on the beach, preparing materials for research, helping with tourist information and merchandise sales, and providing educational activities for local children. Volunteers work up to 40 hours per week and stay in either Lacaco or Boa Esperanca beach camps or with community members in Fundo das Figueras/Norte, with each having a slightly different range of activities. Volunteers on beach patrol always have a staff member or community member along.

Volunteers live in remote communities without nightlife and shops and with a limited variety of food. Volunteers have free time during the day to catch up on sleep (since patrols take place at night), walk and explore the island, or just relax. They take an active part in camp and house maintenance, cleaning and cooking. A volunteer fee covers food (three meals a day) and drinks, transportation from Boavista International Airport to the camp, shared accommodation in tents (those desiring more privacy may bring their own tent), training, and on-site support by the TF team.

More information:
Turtle Foundation: turtle-foundation.org, volunteers@turtle-foundation .org

How to help:

Make a donation, either financial or of equipment; adopt a turtle, nest, or even a ranger; become a member of the Turtle Foundation; purchase a turtle souvenir; or go on a turtle-watching tour guided by the Turtle Foundation, since tour operators make a donation on behalf of every tourist: turtle-foundation.org/Waystohelp/tabid/81/language/en-US/Default.aspx.

Other things to do in the area:

Harbor. Tour the old harbor quay and boatyard.

Water sports. Swim and snorkel from the beaches, particularly Praia de Santa Monica in the south of Boa Vista, considered by many to be Cape Verde's most beautiful beach.

Rocha Estância. Visit this observation point.

Bird-watching. The Cape Verde Islands have four unique species of bird—the Cape Verde sparrow and swift, endangered raso lark, and Cape Verde warbler. Birds that can be seen regularly include magnificent frigatebirds, Cape Verde petrel, grey-headed kingfisher, helmeted guineafowl, brown booby, and red-billed tropicbird.

Whale watching. Take a whale-watching tour. Humpback whales pass through here on seasonal migrations, and the Cape Verde Islands are one of the species' two North Atlantic breeding sites, with the peak breeding season in March and April.

Sal

The Cape Verdean island of Sal has volcanic peaks, salt flats, more than 4 miles of white beaches, and a culture that melds African, Caribbean, Brazilian, and Portuguese influences.

Loggerheads lay nests on Sal from June through October, with nests hatching up until December. Turtles face serious threats here, including hunting for meat and eggs and removal of beach sand for building and unregulated development. The SOS Tartarugas conservation program offers turtle talks during nesting season, which sometimes include night walks on nesting beaches or hatchling releases. Visit the organization's hatchery at Riu Beach to find out about these talks, or you may be able to inquire at your hotel.

SOS Tartarugas hires staff and volunteer Turtle Rangers for four to six months during nesting season but also accepts applications for as little as several weeks, and in peak season, visitors at area hotels can volunteer for even a few days. Rangers receive about a week of initial training, live in a small hostel known as the Turtle House, and prepare group meals in the on-site kitchen.

Rangers regularly patrol Costa Fragata beach near the Turtle House, and a group camps out for five nights at a time to patrol Serra Negra, a national park some distance away. The presence of rangers helps prevent slaughter of nesting turtles; the first year of SOS Tartarugas's operation, some 90 loggerheads were known to have been killed here, but only 6 were killed in 2011. Rangers also sometimes take eggs to secure corrals to protect them from poachers, predators, and light pollution, which can cause hatchlings to head away from rather than toward the ocean, where they may be run over by cars, eaten, or die from dehydration.

Most at-risk nests are brought to the main hatchery, located on the beach of the Riu Resort, where rangers give turtle talks for tourists and host hatchling releases. Visitors can also adopt a nest in the hatchery, a hatchling, or an adult loggerhead turtle. Rangers also, when possible, lead tourists on night walks to witness nesting turtles. Sometimes they find a slaughtered turtle instead, which also presents an educational opportunity.

In 2013, the project recorded a total of 2,585 nests (an increase from 1,037 in 2009). On the beaches it protects, only two suspected deaths of turtles occurred. On the northern beaches, however, 55 turtles were killed in a newly discovered nesting area. Plans are under way to locate a camp there to help solve the problem. That year, rangers also moved 313 threatened nests containing 25,961 eggs to the hatchery, where 19,651 turtles were born, a hatching success rate of 75.7 percent. Average hatching success on the beaches was slightly higher at 78.8 percent.

More information:
SOS Tartarugas: sostartarugas.org/SOSTartarugas/Welcome.html
Apply to be a seasonal Turtle Ranger: turtleconservationjobs.blogspot.
   com/

How to help:
Participate in turtle talks and walks, donate to SOS Tartarugas, or

adopt a nest or hatchlings. Let your hotel or resort know that the sea turtles are one of the reasons you visited Cape Verde.

Other things to do in the area:

Water sports. Scuba dive in the warm Atlantic Ocean around Sal (find out more at caboverdediving.net), or snorkel, fish, sail, or kite board, especially in winter. From January to March, migrating humpback whales pass by the island.

Pedra De Lume. Visit the picturesque salt pans at Pedra De Lume, on the floor of an extinct volcanic crater. Seawater filters up through the crater's fissured rock, filling the pans and providing a natural source of salt. Other sights to see are Algodeiro, a small oasis; and Buracona, a stunningly blue natural tide pool.

Fishing. There is good fishing close to the old lighthouse in Fiura.

Gabon

Gabon hosts one of the world's oldest human settlements and many iconic wild animals, including gorillas, chimpanzees, elephants, and mandrills on land and humpback whales, sea turtles, and manatees along its coast. This country has been relatively isolated, but that is changing, and the country's wildlife faces the threat of increasing industrial development. Gabon established 13 national parks in 2002 that cover roughly 10 percent of the country, and work is ongoing to make these protected areas true refuges for wildlife.

Gabon hosts the highest density of leatherback nests in Africa, representing possibly as much as 30 percent of the global population of this species. Olive ridleys also nest on the coast of Gabon and spend time in the waters offshore from Gabon south to Angola. The Gabon Sea Turtle Partnership, founded in 2005, includes NGOs such as the World Wildlife Fund (WWF) Gabon, Wildlife Conservation Society (WCS), Aventures Sans Frontières, Ibonga, and PROTOMAC and government organizations such as the Gabon National Parks Agency and National Center for Oceanographic Data. The partnership oversees and coordinates sea turtle research and conservation throughout the country and has long-term monitoring and nesting research at four sites: Pongara and Cap-Estérias near Libreville, Gamba, and Mayumba. Gabon's turtle nesting season falls between October and March.

WWF Gabon coordinates fieldwork in the Gamba area. In 2013, from October to the end of March, the organization had a team of six researchers on two beaches, conducting nightly patrols to tag and measure nesting turtles and morning track counts to monitor number and species of nesters. While there is no formal mechanism for volunteers to participate, during the season when staffing and logistics allow, visitors can pay a fee to spend a night camping on one of the beaches with the teams and accompany them on night patrols and morning track counts. The Gabonese team of researchers, generally all male, speak only French, and you will be roughing it, cooking over open fires, and washing in lagoons. Volunteer and tourism opportunities at the other research sites coordinated by the Gabon Turtle Partnership are not formally organized, and any potential participation would be under similarly remote and spartan conditions. Consider it an adventure!

Pongara National Park, a 20-minute boat ride across the estuary from Libreville, contains sandy beaches, savanna, and forest. The Pongara Ecomuseum, adjacent to the beach, offers guided night turtle walks. Bring a turtle-friendly flashlight and keep a respectful distance.

More information:

Gabon Sea Turtle Partnership: seaturtle.org/groups/gabon/home.html

World Wildlife Fund Gabon: wwf-congobasin.org

To inquire about volunteering on the Gamba beaches, contact Gianna Minton, WWF Gabon Marine Coordinator: gminton@wwfcarpo .org.

Wildlife Conservation Society: wcs.org/where-we-work/africa/gabon .aspx

How to help:

If you stay in an area hotel, ask what the property is doing to help sea turtles. Before ordering seafood in area restaurants, ask whether it was purchased from shrimp trawlers using TEDs. WWF, WCS, the University of Exeter, and US NOAA have been working with the Gabonese government testing the use of these devices in the country. Avoid purchasing seafood caught on longlines. Do not ride ATVs on the beach, and take reusable shopping bags rather than single-use plastic bags. Pack out all trash.

🐢 *Ghana*

Formed from a former British colony of the Gold Coast and Togoland trust territory, Ghana became the first sub-Saharan country in colonial Africa to gain its independence, in 1957. It lies on the western coast of Africa, bordering the Gulf of Guinea. Ghana's official language is English, and the United States and Ghana share a long history. The country has a stable government as well as a rich and diverse culture and history and equally diverse wildlife and habitats. Olive ridley, green, and leatherback sea turtles nest on its tropical beaches. In 2012, a loggerhead nest was recorded here for the first time since the 1960s.

Ada Foah and Winneba

Ada Foah, a coastal town in eastern Ghana, has experienced intense erosion, and a years-long sea defense project has limited scientific surveys and ecotourism opportunities. However, the dredging company worked with Phil Allman, a sea turtle researcher at Florida Gulf Coast University, to train local community members to conduct nesting surveys and collect data needed to help minimize effects on sea turtles during the project.

Volunteer opportunities are not currently available while the beach area is an active construction area, but volunteers may be accepted once the project completes, which is anticipated to happen in 2014 or 2015. Volunteers will help survey roughly 6 miles of beach where about 300 leatherbacks and 200 olive ridleys nest from October through February. Peak season runs December through early January. This project works closely with the Ghana Wildlife Division.

Near the historic fishing town of Winneba in central Ghana, a senior wildlife officer who did graduate work through the University of Ghana and trained at Ada Foah, Andrew Agyekumhene, has established a conservation project in collaboration with Allman. Poaching has been a

Sea Turtle Conservation:
Not All Programs Are Created Equal

THIS guide stresses how important it is for conservation and tourism projects to put the best interests of sea turtles and local communities first. Not all projects do so. Some seek first and foremost to make a profit, often at the expense of the animals and habitat. There is nothing wrong with making a profit, of course, and everyone needs to make a living. But there are proven models where local communities can generate income without exploiting sea turtles or people.

Scientists conducting research in Ghana report that many hotel owners advertise nesting sea turtles at "their" beaches. Some have hired people to build hatcheries and move eggs from nesting beaches to these hotel hatcheries, solely to ensure that guests can see turtles. These hotels are often owned by foreign investors, not locals, and operate hatcheries without government permits or expertise. Some foreign NGOs also do similar work without permits and without providing real benefit to the local communities. Advertisements for volunteer positions include requiring that volunteers pay in advance for accommodation and food, provided at a particular hotel the NGO works for or owns.

Those familiar with sea turtle conservation work in Ghana highly recommend that if you are interested in volunteering with sea turtle projects, choose one that works directly through the Ghana Wildlife Division (GWD). The GWD is equivalent to the US Fish and Wildlife Service and is the only authority for sea turtle protection in the country. The agency works through the community, involving local residents in decisions made regarding management of resources. ■

problem here, but nesting surveys have already served to reduce it. The project hires local community members and international interns to survey about 3 miles of beach, with approximately 100 olive ridley and 50 leatherback nests recorded from November through February. Volunteers are welcome but must commit to at least a month.

This project, which works closely with the Ghana Wildlife Division and community leaders in Winneba and Mankoadze, seeks to improve sea turtle conservation by promoting research and monitoring, community education, and ecotourism development. Volunteers will have an opportunity to participate in education programs, fisher workshops, ecotourism promotion, and sea turtle nest monitoring.

More information:
Ghana Wildlife Division: wildlifeghana.com/
To volunteer: contact Phillip Allman, pallman@fgcu.edu; or Andy
    Agyekumhene, andyaohene@yahoo.com

How to help:
    Visit and support only projects operating with appropriate authority from the Ghana Wildlife Division. On area beaches, always follow turtle-safe practices.

🦃 *Kenya, Watamu Turtle Program*

Watamu and Malindi Marine Parks and Reserve cover 88 square miles with about 18 miles of coastline and are part of a United Nations Biosphere Reserve that also includes the Arabuko Sokoke Forest. A reef stretches the length of the coast, forming several lagoons rich in coral and fish species, and there are also numerous patch reefs. The reserve provides an important residing and feeding habitat for sea turtles; the beach within Watamu Marine National Park and Reserve is a key turtle nesting ground.

Watamu Turtle Watch, formed in 1997 by a local naturalist, became Local Ocean Trust, a registered charitable trust, which works in close cooperation with the Kenya Wildlife Service, Fisheries Department, Kenya Marine Fisheries Research Institute, and the Kenya Sea Turtle Conservation Committee, of which it is a member.

Volunteers sign up for four to eight weeks from March through December to conduct nightly beach patrols during nesting season, carry out posthatching nest excavations, assist with turtle releases and data collection, and help feed and care for turtles in rehabilitation. They also help with education and outreach and community development. Accommodation is provided in Lallies House, up to two volunteers to a room, each with a toilet, sink and shower, and electricity.

The house also has two large outdoor covered areas, a communal dining area, and a large communal kitchen with refrigerator and microwave. It is near the main office and rehabilitation center and a five-minute walk from the beach. The weekly fee covers lunch on weekdays (volunteers prepare their other meals in the kitchen), accommodation, cleaning, airport transfers from Malindi, training and supervision, and use of bicycles. Laundry can be done at minimal extra cost.

More information:
Working Abroad: workingabroad.com/page/180/watamu-turtles-kenya
    .htm, victoria.mcneil@workingabroad.com

How to help:
Purchase local crafts and use local restaurants, hotels, and other services whenever possible.

Other things to do in the area:
Water sports. Watamu is part of a United Nations Biosphere Reserve, with beautiful beaches and a coral reef that provides excellent snorkeling and diving. Various water sports, glass-bottom boat tours, and deep-sea fishing are available in the area.

Gede ruins. Visit the some of the oldest ruins in the country, in dense forest.

Kipepeo Butterfly Farm. Visit the farm next to the Gede Museum.

Hiking. Hike nature trails in Arabuko Sokoke Forest, the largest remaining tract of indigenous coastal forest in East Africa and the second most important in terms of biodiversity and endemic species in all of Africa.

Mozambique

This former Portuguese colony in southeastern Africa, between South Africa and Tanzania, gained independence in 1975. The country has 1,534 miles of coastline bordering the Indian Ocean and a tropical to subtropical climate. Loggerhead, green, leatherback, hawksbill, and olive ridley sea turtles make use of Mozambique's coastal and marine ecosystems as feeding, breeding, and nesting grounds.

Ponta do Ouro Partial Marine Reserve at the border with South

Africa is the largest rookery in the country, with about 700 loggerhead and leatherback nests per season. People from local communities have run a monitoring and tagging program here since 1995 and may eventually offer turtle-watching tours.

Bazaruto Archipelago National Park covers 540 square miles and five islands, sheltering East Africa's largest population of threatened dugongs, as well as sea turtles. It is a year-round feeding ground for juvenile greens but has a relatively small number of nests per season. The nesting grounds are on the eastern side of the islands, while resorts face the mainland. Given the combination of distance and low number of nests, there are currently no turtle tour operations here.

Quirimbas National Park, 2,900 square miles including 11 islands in the Quirimbas Archipelago, contains an abundance of fish and rare marine species, such as dugongs and whales, and five species of sea turtles. The major threats to turtles here are loss and degradation of habitats; overexploitation of eggs, meat, and other products; and incidental capture by trawlers, gillnets, and other fishing gear. The World Wildlife Fund has supported marine turtle conservation in Africa since 1969. Nests are few and far between, and there is currently no monitoring program and therefore no volunteer opportunities.

Vamizi Island, in the Quirimbas Archipelago off the northern coast of Mozambique, sees roughly 200 to 250 green sea turtle nests between December and March each year, and 3 to 5 hawksbill nests. The Malaune Project began turtle monitoring and nest protection here in 2003 and opened the Vamizi Island Lodge in 2005. In 2010, the project joined forces with the WWF. Rangers patrol nearly 7 miles of beach each morning, recording false crawls and taking GPS coordinates and marking nests. At the end of the incubation period, nests are checked daily. After one has hatched, patrollers count the shells and undeveloped and unhatched eggs. Any live hatchlings still in the nest are kept in a dark, quiet place until around sunset, then released in front of the lodge bar. These releases present an opportunity to educate guests about sea turtles and the monitoring project.

Guests are also occasionally invited to witness tagging of nesting females on Lighthouse Beach. Every week the lodge offers presentations to guests about its various projects, including the sea turtle project. There is currently not a formal volunteer project, but help is always welcome.

The project is starting a nest relocation project and transferring data to a virtual database and could use volunteers for these efforts. The best time to volunteer is December to March, and depending on the activities, your volunteer stint could last from one or two weeks to two months. Volunteers will stay in one of the staff houses, if space is available, or in a tent.

More information:
Vamizi Island Lodge: vamizi.com

How to help:
Donate to World Wildlife Fund: wwf.panda.org.

🏳 South Africa

Located at the tip of the continent, the Republic of South Africa has more than 1,500 miles of coastline in the Atlantic and Indian Oceans. It contains some of the oldest archeological evidence of human habitation in the world. Loggerhead and leatherback sea turtles nest here, but South Africa's large and growing population contributes to threats to their survival.

iSimangaliso Wetland Park

On the eastern coast near the border with Mozambique, iSimangaliso Wetland Park, listed as a World Heritage Site in December 1999, encompasses more than 820,000 acres. It holds three major lake systems, eight interlinking ecosystems, most of South Africa's remaining swamp forests, the continent's largest estuarine system, 526 bird species, and 25,000-year-old coastal dunes ranking among the highest in the world. The name iSimangaliso means "miracle and wonder."

Loggerhead and leatherback sea turtles nest on the Indian Ocean coastline of the park between October and February, with hatchlings emerging from about January into March. Ezemvelo KZN Wildlife, the provincial conservation authority in partnership with the Wetland Park Authority, has protected this area and monitored nesting for more than 50 years. Camping and lodge accommodations are available in the park.

Hotels and outfitters offer turtle tours to the park from St. Lucia and Cape Vidal, Sodwana Bay, Mabibi, Rocktail Bay, and Bhanga Nek. Tours are scheduled sporadically and take place during the night when the tide is right, which may mean the early hours of the morning. The length of tours depends on how many turtles are encountered and the necessity of leaving the beach before the tide comes back in, but they generally last two to four hours.

More information:
iSimangaliso Wetland Park: 27-35-590-1633 (international call),
   isimangaliso.com/index.php, info@iSimangaliso.com

How to help:
Follow sea turtle–friendly practices on the beach. Stay in local accommodations and hire only trained local guides appointed by the Wetland Park Authority for turtle tours.

Other things to do in the area:
Wildlife viewing. Observe birds and other wildlife on self-guided and guided walking trails or drives, including guided night drives in the Eastern Shores and uMkhuze.
Kayaking. Kayak on Lake St. Lucia or Lake Sibaya.
Horseback riding. Ride horses on St. Lucia's beaches or on the Eastern Shores of False Bay.
Water sports. Deep-sea fish or surf from the beaches, and scuba dive or snorkel in the ocean.

Green sea turtles. *(Top photo © Neil Ever Osborne; www.neileverosborne.com. Bottom photo by Bethany Resnick)*

An olive ridley sea turtle. (Photo by Guillaume Feuillet)

Indian Ocean

⚑ *India*

G REENS, loggerheads, leatherbacks, and hawksbills nest around the Indian Ocean and Arabian Sea at various times throughout most of the year. Olive ridley, green, leatherback, and hawksbill sea turtles are found all along the 4,970-mile coastline of India, including the mainland states of Gujarat, Karnataka, Kerala, Maharashtra, and Goa on the western coast; Orissa, Andhra Pradesh, Tamil Nadu, Puducherry, and West Bengal on the eastern coast; and the Andaman and Nicobar Islands and the Lakshadweep Islands. There is sporadic nesting by olive ridleys along the coast of the mainland, and leatherbacks and greens nest on the islands. Some olive ridleys nest in *arribadas* in parts of India.

Millions of people live along the Indian coast, making nests vulnerable to predation by humans and feral animals, mainly dogs. Artificial lighting frequently disorients hatchlings as well. Conservation efforts here must weigh the costs and benefits of managing nests on the beach against protecting them in hatcheries, with the choice depending on the nature and degree of the threat and the financial and personnel resources available. State forest departments in West Bengal, Orissa, Goa, Gujarat, and Andaman and Nicobar Islands and NGOs in Andhra Pradesh, Kerala, Maharashtra, Karnataka, and Tamil Nadu run hatchery programs.

Kundapura

In the town of Kundapura, on the western coast of Karnataka, Field Services and Intercultural Learning of India operates a sea turtle conservation project. It began in October 2005, when volunteers built Turtle Information Centres and improved nesting habitats on Maravanthe and Bejadi beaches south and north of Kundapura. From August to February, you can volunteer for two to three weeks to build hatcheries and Turtle Information Centres; help with promotional activities; and conduct awareness campaigns at schools, villages, harbors, and fishing communities.

165

As a part of intercultural learning, volunteers stay with local families and also participate in Indian cooking classes, Kannada (language) and other classes, boat trips, and visits to temples. The program fee covers accommodation, food, and local transportation.

More information:

FSL-India: +91-080-22111930, +91-080-22111931 (international calls), fsl-india.org, ltvfslindia@gmail.com

Orissa

The coastline of Orissa, bounded by the Bay of Bengal on the east, stretches nearly 300 miles from West Bengal in the north to Andhra

Pradesh in the south. Olive ridleys nest both sporadically and in *arribadas* (mass nestings), and other species, mostly juvenile greens and hawksbills, occasionally strand or are spotted offshore. *Arribadas* of olive ridleys have been recorded at three beaches in Orissa: Gahirmatha, Rushikulya, and Devi River mouth, although no *arribadas* have been seen at Devi in more than a decade.

These *arribadas* involve 50,000 to 200,000 sea turtles annually. This genetically distinct population may be the original source of the world's other olive ridley populations. In the 1990s, tens of thousands of these sea turtles stranded, representing probably only a fraction of those dying as fisheries bycatch. This could mean a population crash in the future, when hatchlings that those sea turtles would have produced would have begun reproducing themselves.

Sea turtle conservation started here in the mid-1970s, with discovery of the mass nesting beach in Gahirmatha. The Indian Forest Department, Central Marine Fisheries Research Institute, and Utkal University were involved in sea turtle research and conservation for several decades, and a Forest Department researcher discovered the mass nesting beach in Devi mouth. In the 1990s, scientists with the Wildlife Institute of India discovered the mass nesting beach in Rushikulya and tagged thousands of nesting females. This work revealed the extent of turtle mortality in trawl nets and led to renewed conservation efforts. A consortium of organizations, including local conservation groups such as Rushikulya Sea Turtle Protection Committee, Sea Turtle Action Program, and the Orissa Traditional Fish Workers' Union and state and national NGOs, began the Orissa Marine Resources Conservation Consortium (OMRCC), with support from members of Dakshin Foundation and the United Artists' Association.

Wildlife Protection Society of India, Wildlife Society of Orissa, Greenpeace, World Wildlife Fund–India and other groups have worked here to reduce turtle mortality, particularly through enforcement of fishing regulations that prohibit trawlers from operating within 3 miles of the coast and required use of turtle excluder devices (TEDs). Enforcement remains a problem. The OMRCC hopes to encourage cooperation between turtle conservationists and fishers toward their common interest in safeguarding nearshore areas from trawling and maintaining healthy ecosystems.

Arribadas and Sea Turtle Conservation in India

ONE night in December 1988, Kartik Shanker patrolled a beach in Madras on the eastern coast of India looking for sea turtles. Watching an olive ridley crawling ashore to nest inspired him to pursue a career in ecology, and he later helped establish the Students' Sea Turtle Conservation Network, now one of the longest-running sea turtle conservation programs in India. In 1999, while conducting postdoctoral research on sea turtle genetics, the young scientist witnessed his first *arribada* on remote Nasi Island, in the Bay of Bengal off the coast of Orissa.

"The last week of March, we landed at Ekakulanasi on a routine survey," he recalls. "Turtles started to come ashore to nest and kept coming and coming and coming. Thousands and thousands that night and the whole of the next day and the night after that. The next afternoon, we approached Nasi. There was sand flying and thousands of turtles coming ashore, searching amidst a sea of turtles for a site, nesting, and returning to the sea. This lasted nearly a week, and a total of about 180,000 turtles nested on the two islands, a truly astonishing nesting density."

Years later, he still recalls the scene vividly. "Moonlight glinted off the wet backs of the turtles as they came out of the water, thousands of them spread across the beach like a battalion of armored tanks. On the beach, they crawled over each other, their flailing flippers throwing sand indiscriminately over nesting turtles. Many became so covered with sand you could barely see them, just the neck and top of the carapace sticking out of the sand. After the moon went down, it became difficult to walk on the beach, even with a torch. We were weaving across the beach trying to avoid turtles but sooner or later tripping over one."

Now an assistant professor at the Centre for Ecological Sciences, Indian Institute of Science, Bangalore, Shanker has focused for two decades on the biology and conservation of sea turtles, with ongoing projects on olive ridleys in Orissa, leatherbacks in the Andaman and Nicobar Islands, and greens in the Lakshadweep Islands. He has been involved in establishing networks for marine conservation in Orissa and is a founding trustee of the Dakshin Foundation, which informs and advocates for conservation and natural resource management. ∎

Those traveling to the area can arrange visits to nesting beaches by getting in touch with one of the local organizations involved, such as the Rushikulya Sea Turtle Protection Committee, upon arrival in Orissa. Also get in touch if you are interested in volunteering; opportunities are available occasionally, but a more formal program is being considered.

More information:
Sea Turtles of India: seaturtlesofindia.org
Dakshin Foundation: dakshin.org/
Wildlife Protection Society of India: wpsi-india.org/wpsi/index.php

How to help:
Turn off outside lights at night to avoid disorienting hatchlings, and use only turtle-friendly flashlights on the beach at night. Be careful when boating to avoid hitting sea turtles in the water.

🏴 *Oman*

The Sultanate of Oman contains a wealth of biodiversity and miles of unspoiled shoreline on the Sea of Oman, which connects to the Arabian Sea and, beyond it, to the Indian Ocean. Fourteen conservation areas in the country include sanctuaries, nature reserves, and natural parks. Although loggerheads nest throughout the Indian Ocean, the numbers are small except in Oman. For the most part, it is not known whether loggerhead nesting populations in the Indian Ocean are decreasing, increasing, or remaining the same.

Raz al Jinz

The Raz al Jinz Nature Reserve was established in 1996 by merging a smaller nature reserve and the Ras al Hadd scenic reserve, with the intent to better protect sea turtles and their habitat. It covers 46 square miles and 28 miles of coastline.

Ras al Jinz beach is one of the most important nesting habitats for green sea turtles in the world. The reserve offers guided turtle tours to see nesting turtles at night and in the early morning. A visitor center provides educational displays about sea turtles. The Turtle Reserve has 14 rooms with air-conditioning, refrigerators, televisions, and Internet access; lodging includes breakfast and tours. An on-site restaurant serves breakfast, lunch, and dinner.

More information:

Ras al Jinz Nature Reserve: +968-96550606 (international call), rasaljinz-turtlereserve.com, reservations@rasaljinz-turtlereserve.com

How to help:

Clean up all trash and litter on the beach or in the water, and do not drive on the beach or walk in areas around nests. Do not buy any products made from turtles. Road improvements and increased development threaten this nesting population. Let locals know that you came here to observe sea turtles in their natural environment.

Flatback hatchlings entering the ocean on Barrow Island, Western Australia.
(Photos by Kellie Pendoley)

Australian flatback sea turtle, Barrow Island, Western Australia. (Photo by Jarrad Sherborne)

South Pacific

🏳 National Park of American Samoa/National Marine Sanctuary of American Samoa

AMERICAN SAMOA, the only US territory south of the equator, consists of five rugged volcanic islands and two coral atolls, a total of 76 square miles of land. The 13,500-acre National Park of American Samoa takes in three islands—Tutuila, Ofu, and Ta'u—with rain forest on the mountains and beaches on the coast. Coral fringing reefs of the park shelter the greatest marine biodiversity in the United States and its possessions, with more than 950 native fish and 250 coral species.

Only a small number of turtles nest on Ofu; 12 nests were recorded during the 2013 season (September to May), representing four to six individuals. There are four identified nesting beaches on the island: Vaoto, Toaga, Asaga, and Mafafa. Records exist of nesting in Olosega Island, but this is rare. Greens and hawksbills forage and feed on the reefs around Ofu and Olosega.

The park has a homestay program on all three islands, and there are hotels on Tutuila. Snorkeling or scuba diving (note that gear and air can be difficult to obtain) in the park offer the possibility of spotting sea turtles swimming or foraging. Rangers present programs on sea turtles for local schools but do not have the resources to provide them for tourists. You are most likely to see turtles out on the reefs.

American Samoa also has two designated National Marine Sanctuaries—National Marine Sanctuary of American Samoa and the Rose Atoll Marine National Monument, which is accessible only for scientific research. Fagatele Bay, located in the National Marine Sanctuary of American Samoa on Tutuila Island, is home to a wide variety of animals and plants, including hawksbill and green sea turtles. The bay can be accessed from the village of Futiga Monday to Friday, 7:30 a.m. to 4:00 p.m., and Saturday, 7:30 a.m. to 1:30 p.m. There is no charge, but visitors are asked to register at the gate. Sanctuary educational staff participate in programs

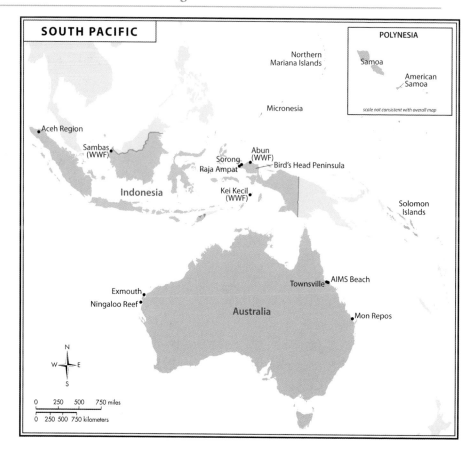

such as Earth Day, Arbor Week, and Coastweeks. Check the website for scheduled events.

More information:
National Park of American Samoa: 684-633-7082, ext. 22, nps.gov/npsa
National Marine Sanctuary of American Samoa: 684-633-6500, americansamoa.noaa.gov/

How to help:
Make a donation to the park.

Other things to do in the area:

Explore the area. The park is relatively new and very remote, so you will not find the usual national park facilities common on the mainland. But explore secluded villages, observe tropical forest plants and wildlife, snorkel coral reefs, and enjoy magnificent island and sea vistas.

Homestay program. Sleep in a Samoan house, or *fale*, with a Samoan family, and participate in village activities, including cutting pandanus (laufala) tree leaves and drying them to weave mats: nps.gov/npsa/historyculture/homestay.htm.

🏴 *Australia*

Mon Repos, Queensland

Loggerhead, flatback, and green sea turtles nest along the central Queensland coast from November through March. Mon Repos Conservation Park, about a four-and-a-half hour drive north from Brisbane, hosts the largest concentration of nesting on the eastern Australian mainland and the most significant nesting population of the endangered loggerhead turtle in the South Pacific Ocean region. November to March, the Queensland Parks and Wildlife Service offers nightly guided Turtle Encounter tours; November to January are best to see nesting, and January to the end of March are best to see hatchlings.

From mid-October through April, public beach access is restricted from 6:00 p.m. to 6:00 a.m. to protect nesting turtles and hatchlings. Turtle Encounters are offered from November to late March. Tours begin at 7:00 p.m. in the Mon Repos Information Centre with a review of recent research and turtle displays. Some nights turtles arrive late, so be prepared to wait up to six hours before a turtle is spotted and your group escorted to the beach, and recognize that sometimes turtles do not show up. Rangers also give talks in the outdoor amphitheater on sea turtles and turtle-watching guidelines. Youngsters can join in Junior Turtle Ranger activities during the evening. Entry fees support conservation and protection of the sea turtles.

More information:

Mon Repos Conservation Park: nprsr.qld.gov.au/parks/mon-repos/
  index.html

Book tours in advance: in person at 271 Bourbong Street, Bundaberg;
  07-4153-8888 (international call), bookbundabergregion.com.au

How to help:

Help prevent disorientation of nesting sea turtles and hatchlings by
turning off all outdoor lights and closing blinds after dark.

Other things to do in the area:

Outdoor activities. The park offers hiking and cycling, with several
natural tracks and a 4-mile cycling trail; swimming, with lifeguards on
duty 9:00 a.m. to 5:00 p.m. during school holidays; and boating. Camping
is not allowed in the park, but accommodations, including camping, are
available in nearby Bargara and Bundaberg.

Ningaloo Reef, Western Australia

Ningaloo Marine Park runs 180 miles along the western coast of Australia and is part of the Ningaloo Coast World Heritage site. This is one
of the most important sea turtle nesting areas in the Indian Ocean, which
was a key reason for its World Heritage listing. Three species, green, loggerhead, and hawksbill, nest on mainland beaches and islands of Ningaloo Reef during the summer months from November to March. In 2002,
the Department of Environment and Conservation (DEC), Cape Conservation Group (CCG), Murdoch University, and World Wildlife Fund
Australia developed the Ningaloo Turtle Program to help conserve marine turtles and their habitats. The program is now operated during each
turtle nesting season as a collaborative effort between DEC and CCG.

The program provides an opportunity for local community, interstate,
and international volunteers to take part in turtle conservation. Volunteers are needed between December and January to monitor nesting
beaches and record activity along the beaches of the North West Cape.
A typical day begins at 5:30 a.m. with approximately four or five hours
of data collection on the beach. The rest of the day is free to explore the
Ningaloo Coast and Exmouth township, travel inland to see spectacular

gorges in Cape Range National Park, or catch up on sleep. Other volunteer duties include entering data, camping within the Cape Range National Park to monitor an isolated loggerhead turtle rookery, and assisting with turtle rescues as required.

The DEC also helped set up other community monitoring programs and implemented and manages the Jurabi Turtle Centre, an interpretive education facility designed to educate visitors about appropriate behavior around turtles. During each turtle nesting season, DEC runs educational Turtle Interaction Evenings. Visitors to the park can see marine turtles nesting from approximately November to March and turtle hatchlings from January until May.

More information:
Ningaloo Turtle Program: ningalooturtles.org.au

How to help:
Follow the Turtle Code of Conduct for sea turtle watchers, available on the Ningaloo Turtle Program website under "Turtle Toolbox." Do not drive on known turtle rookery beaches during the nesting season, use reusable shopping bags, and dispose of all trash carefully (especially when boating). Boycott any turtle products you encounter overseas.

Other things to do in the area:
Marine Park activities. Take advantage of boating, coral viewing, kayaking, snorkeling and fishing in the shallow lagoon behind the reef, and sightseeing flights.

Viewing sea life. See whale sharks from March to July, manta rays June to October, humpback whales and calves June to November, in addition to sea turtles year-round.

Sea Turtle Foundation, North Queensland

The Sea Turtle Foundation, founded by a group of sea turtle biologists and volunteers as the Indo-Pacific Sea Turtle Conservation Group in 2001, seeks to address research gaps and threats to sea turtles in northern Queensland. The organization focuses on three areas: research, education, and action.

Female flatback sea turtle on the intertidal flats just off of the east coast of Barrow Island, Western Australia. (Photo by Kellie Pendoley)

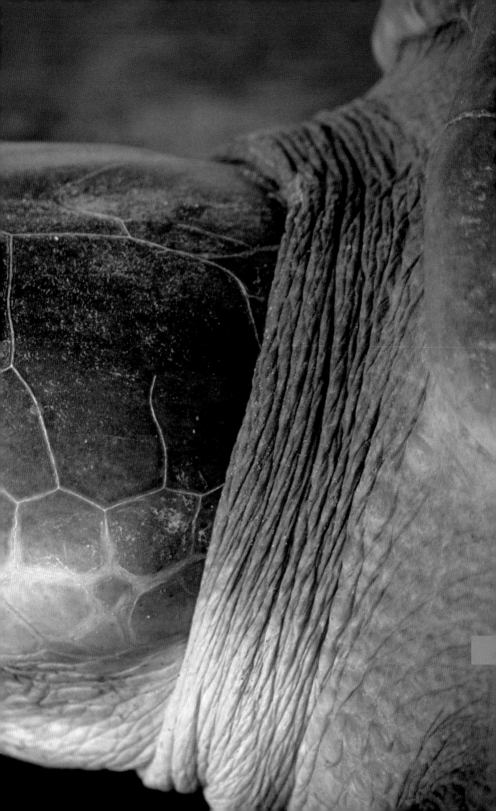

Research projects include monitoring of nesting at AIMS Beach, 21 miles south of Townsville; collecting data on climate change impacts on hawksbill turtles on Milman Island, northern Great Barrier Reef; and monitoring of internesting patterns and migration pathways of green turtles at Raine Island.

During nesting season, in November and December, visitors can help on monitoring patrols at AIMS Beach, where turtles are measured and tag numbers recorded. Nest protectors designed to stop feral animals from digging up and eating eggs are sometimes placed around nests. Monitoring is timed to coincide with a high tide around dusk, when most turtles come ashore to nest. Groups are led by an expert and limited to 10 people, with priority given to foundation members and supporters, which anyone can become with a monthly donation of $10 or more, or you can make a one-time donation to secure a place. Given the beach's remote location, it is not possible to leave early, and age restrictions apply.

Volunteers can help in a variety of other ways. "Casual volunteers" can just stop by briefly to help with beach cleanup events, staff a stall at community events, or help with administrative work in the office. Education officers, who must have a Blue Card and a background in sea turtle biology, give interactive talks about sea turtles and dangers facing them to schools and community groups. School-talk assistants help education officers present to primary school children and also must have a Blue Card. (A Blue Card is a way to screen and monitor those working with children and young people and is intended to minimize the risk of harm to children.) Other volunteers help develop workshop materials or write lesson plans and presentations, and graphic designers can help with educational materials. Volunteers are always needed during sponsored swims, sausage sizzles, garage sales, school events, and other events used to raise funds for the organization.

More information:

Sea Turtle Foundation: seaturtlefoundation.org/volunteer/ (under "Education Officer," click on "Blue Card" to link to a Blue Card application)

How to help:

Become a member or supporter of the foundation, make a donation,

or purchase sea turtle–related gear from its website: seaturtlefoundation
.org/gifts-and-gear/.

🐢 *Commonwealth of the Northern Mariana Islands*

The Commonwealth of the Northern Mariana Islands (CNMI), one
of two commonwealths in the United States (the other is Puerto Rico),
includes 15 islands in the western Pacific Ocean about three-quarters of
the way between Hawai'i and the Philippines.

Green, hawksbill, and leatherback sea turtles, which are called *ihaggan*
in the local Chamorro language, forage in the waters around the islands.
While once plentiful throughout the archipelago, the nesting population
has been severely depleted by harvest. CNMI Department of Lands and
Natural Resources, Guam Department of Aquatic and Wildlife Resources, Pacific Marine Resources Institute (PMRI), and local volunteers are
working to recover Mariana Islands sea turtle populations.

Nearshore habitats contain mostly juvenile sea turtles that, once ma-
ture, will migrate to Asia or other Pacific Island nations to nest. Research
focuses on understanding the dynamics of sea turtle populations, their
connectivity with regional populations, and their ecology. The project is
working to protect nesting habitat and build community involvement in
sea turtle conservation.

If you dive, boat, or visit the shore here, you will quite likely see a
turtle. Banzai Cliff and the Bird Island overlook on Saipan are good places
to catch a glimpse from shore, and divers in Laolao Bay are often joined
by turtles. The project is still working to establish a formal volunteer program, but visitors to the area can inquire about opportunities to help protect nesting turtles and nests.

More information:
CNMI Sea Turtle Conservation Program, Pacific Marine Resources Institute:
   670-664-6026, pacmares.com/Home.html, info@pacmares.com
Sea Turtles of the Mariana Islands: ihaggan.com/Welcome.html

How to help:
   Harassing or catching turtles is a crime in CNMI. If you witness this
behavior, call CRIMESTOPPERS at 670-234-7272.

Practice responsible turtle-watching behavior (find a helpful guide at coral.org/files/pdf/guides/turtle_watching_english.pdf), and report sightings via e-mail to david.benavente@crm.gov.mp.

Use grills to cook on the beach, rather than fires directly on the sand, which can kill hatchlings. If you go fishing, use barbless circle hooks, which are less likely to hook a sea turtle, and use fish as bait rather than squid.

Other things to do in the area:

Water sports. Snorkel or scuba dive the incredible coral reefs.

 **Indonesia**

Indonesia is an archipelago of more than 17,000 islands, stretching from Sumatra in the Indian Ocean to New Guinea in the South Pacific through a number of smaller seas. The world's fourth-most-populous country, it neighbors Papua New Guinea, Malaysia, the Philippines, and Australia. It is in this chapter because most of the sea turtle conservation work taking place in Indonesia happens on islands on the Pacific side. Leatherback, hawksbill, green, and olive ridley sea turtles nest throughout Indonesia, and flatbacks and loggerheads forage in its waters.

Aceh Region

Yayasan Pulau Banyak, a local nongovernmental organization, was started in 1994 to provide alternative income for communities in the Aceh region through small-scale tourism. The program was halted in 2001 but revived in 2006. Local community members were trained to conduct beach patrols and tag turtles beginning in 2008. Tagging data show that Pulau Banyak's nesting population is very important for Indonesia but also for other parts of the world. The organization's programs include ecotourism development and other education and training for residents, an environmental education program to raise awareness about coral reefs, rain forests, and the importance of sea turtles.

Yayasan Pulau Banyak needs volunteers to assist in beach monitoring on the island of Bangkaru. Duties include nightly beach patrols to collect data on the nesting population, morning patrols, and environmental education. Volunteers who are students may collect data on the nesting population for their own research or fill a school or university practical placement. The organization also needs volunteers willing to teach English in the local community.

Volunteers receive training and briefing material, basic but comfortable accommodations, and food in an idyllic location with abundant marine and terrestrial wildlife—and spare time to snorkel or enjoy the uninhabited island. The organization will arrange visa and transport to and from the site and between islands. An administrative fee is charged for this service, as well as a monthly fee for food and lodging and to support the project. A minimum commitment of two weeks is required.

More information:
Yayasan Pulau Banyak: acehturtleconservation.org
To volunteer: contact the volunteer coordinator, maggiemuurmans@
     gmail.com

How to help:
Make a donation to support the project at "How you can help" on the website.

Bird's Head Peninsula, Jamursba Medi

On the northern coast of the Bird's Head Peninsula on Papua, leatherbacks that forage off the coast of Washington, Oregon, and California in summer nest on beaches of Jamursba Medi and Warmon from April to September. This remote corner of the planet has no roads or landing strips, and the nearest small village is more than 7 miles away. But the population of nesting leatherbacks remains one of the largest in the Pacific basin, and there is a concerted effort at the site to protect the species.

A research and monitoring camp is located at Batu Rumah beach in Jamursba Medi, and for the six-month season, teams from the Bird's Head Leatherback Conservation and Research Program, State University of Papua (BHL-UNIPA), and local villagers patrol the beaches for nesting turtles, which are measured and tagged. Visitors can go on Turtle

Watch tours here, by first acquiring a permit at the offices of Tambrauw Government in Sausapor or the Natural Resources Conservation Bureau in Sorong (permits cannot be obtained or guide fees paid on-site). Representatives of these offices then inform the BHL-UNIPA project of the number of permits issued so on-site staff can plan for the visits. Visitors arrive by boat at an anchoring point off Batu Rumah beach. Tours last two and one-half to three hours and include observing nesting turtles when they are present and discussion of sea turtle biology and conservation and of the flora, fauna, geology, and geography of the area. No inappropriate flashlights, pets, or unauthorized photography are allowed, and insect repellent is recommended.

More information:
Bird's Head Leatherback Conservation and Research Program, State
    University of Papua: bhlunipa@yahoo.co.id

How to help:
    Visit only with the proper authorization and on approved tours. Do not litter on the beach or in the water.

Raja Ampat, West Papua

In 2002, conservation scientists first visited the island of Piai, in northwestern Raja Ampat, West Papua, and recognized it as a potentially significant nesting location for green sea turtles. On a return trip in 2005 to tag sea turtles, the scientists noticed that the rookery suffered intense poaching pressure. Conservation International–Indonesia sponsored a local NGO, Papua Sea Turtle Foundation, or Yayasan Penyu Papua to start a conservation project. Starting in December 2006, men from local clans patrolled beaches and collected nesting data, essentially eliminating poaching in the process.

More information:
Ocean Positive: oceanpositive.org

How to help:
    Make a donation to Ocean Positive online.

World Wildlife Fund Indonesia

The World Wildlife Fund (WWF) works throughout Indonesia in addition to the Burau Archipelago, which has one of South Asia's largest nesting and feeding populations of green sea turtles. At least 15,000 greens nest on these islands annually, with nesting activity peaking May to August. WWF's field program aims to reduce poaching by issuing fewer government concession permits for harvest, decreasing fishing-related mortality by establishing fishing cooperatives, and managing nesting sites in cooperation with local organizations.

Kei Kecil, a small archipelago north of Australia, contains leatherback foraging habitat, with activity particularly during July to November and March and April. The abundance of turtles here attracts photographers and has stirred interest in development of ecotourism in the area. For generations, a clan of Kei islanders have hunted leatherbacks and considered them sacred food. WWF has been working with local governments and communities to develop a marine protected area (MPA) with no-take zones to help protect the turtle population, regulate the traditional harvest, and promote marine tourism.

Paloh Beach, Sambas, also hosts a large population of nesting greens and hawksbills, with recent data showing more than 3,000 green sea turtle nests annually. WWF is working to establish another MPA here as well as to transform egg poachers into monitoring and surveillance workers on nesting beaches.

The largest leatherback nesting population in the western Pacific is found in Abun, West Papua. These same turtles migrate to California and along the US West Coast at other times of the year. Working with West Papua's Natural Resources Conservation Agency and the University of Papua, WWF started a field conservation program to protect nests on Jamursba Medi, which has three important leatherback nesting beaches totaling about 13 miles, and Warmon, to the west, with about 4 miles of beaches. Some 500 females nest here annually, with peak season running June to August. Since 1995, some protection has been afforded by controlling feral animals in the area, although changes in government officials and other delays mean protected areas are not yet large enough or adequately enforced. WWF continues to collate information and lobby with different groups for an appropriate turtle-based MPA. The organization also works with community groups on incentives for conservation.

Visitors to any of these islands or communities during nesting season may be fortunate enough to witness a sea turtle nesting or a nest hatching, or to encounter adult, juvenile, or hatchling sea turtles in the water. If you are one of those lucky people, remember to practice responsible wildlife watching. Visitors can often join WWF field teams at work as well.

More information:
World Wildlife Fund: wwf.panda.org/what_we_do/endangered_
    species/marine_turtles/ and wwf.panda.org/what_we_do/
    endangered_species/marine_turtles/asian_marine_turtles/
    our_solutions/

How to help:
Donate to WWF's work through "Send a Turtle to Rehab" at shop. panda.org/turtle-rehab.html. Do not buy products made from sea turtles. Support well-managed sea turtle conservation-based tourism. According to the WWF report *Money Talks: Economic Aspects of Marine Turtle Use and Conservation*, sensitively planned and operated tourism activities can generate three times as much income for local communities as slaughtering turtles for meat or consuming their eggs. Download the report at wwf.panda.org/about_our_earth/all_publications/?153802/ wwwpandaorglacmarineturtlespublications#.

📑 *Ulithi Sea Turtle Project, Micronesia*

Ulithi Atoll, a cluster of islets just north of the equator in the western portion of the Pacific, is one of the outer island groups about 100 miles northeast of Yap State, part of the Federated States of Micronesia. Two hundred miles of coral reefs and low islets provide important feeding and nesting grounds for green sea turtles. Leatherbacks have been reported in deep waters around the atoll, and olive ridleys outside the reef of Yap Proper. Locals report that hawksbills forage on the reef.

All islands and reefs in Ulithi are privately held, and activities occur only by permission of landowner chiefs. At the invitation of those chiefs, the Oceanic Society initiated a program in 2005 on the island of Loosiep, one of five islands known as Turtle Islands and identified as significant green sea turtle nesting sites. Two of them, Gielop and Iar, are believed to be the largest green turtle rookery in Micronesia. Harvest of eggs, juveniles, and adult turtles had led to the decline of the number of sea turtles here, and nesting turtles also face threats from marine debris, commercial fisheries, and water pollution.

The program supports the Ulithi Sea Turtle Conservation Project, which trains local residents to conduct sea turtle research and monitoring. Since 2005, trained Falalop community members have tagged hundreds of turtles and collected nest ecology data to determine turtle distribution, peak nesting season, and relative reproductive success. In the 1990s, a satellite tracking effort was launched.

The society offers trips to participate in the monitoring project. The trip begins with a briefing in Yap, followed by a half-day snorkeling the coral reef and an overnight stay in thatched-roof cabanas with air-conditioning, ceiling fans, refrigerators, and private verandas. Volunteers travel to Ulithi and stay in a beachfront lodge, also with air-conditioning, that serves as a base for monitoring surveys on outlying islands. Meals are served family style in a dining room. At the Loosiep field camp, volunteers stay in local-style huts and eat locally prepared meals picnic style. Volunteers participate in beach patrols at night and in the early morning to look for nesting turtles and collect biological data and may help rescue hatchlings stuck in collapsed nests or conduct other tasks as needed.

Free time can be spent bird-watching or snorkeling on the island's reef. The group has the opportunity to meet with community members to learn about cultural traditions and local crafts as well.

More information:
Oceanic Society: 415-256-9604 or 800-326-7491, oceanicsociety.org/
    conservation/ulithi-sea-turtle-project
For information on volunteer trips: ExpeditionManager@
    oceanicsociety.org

How to help:
Donations to the society can be directed specifically to the Ulithi project.

🐢 *Samoa*

Samoa includes 10 volcanic islands in the South Pacific roughly half-way between New Zealand and Hawai'i. Reefs around the island contain 200 types of coral and an abundance of marine life, including sea turtles.

Samoan folklore gives sea turtles the power to save fishers lost at sea, and perhaps because of this, the Samoan word for sea turtle, *i'a sa*, translates as "sacred fish." Samoans traditionally harvested sea turtles for food and used the shell to make bracelets, combs, and fishing hooks and in ceremonial headpieces. Turtles appear in Samoan songs and art, and there are turtle petroglyphs on the islands. Greens and hawksbills are the most common around Samoa.

The Samoan Web Ambassadors Programme (SWAP), a Samoan registered charitable trust founded by a New Zealand entrepreneur, Dennis A. Smith, was established to encourage post-tsunami tourism in the country. The organization works with tourism businesses in Samoa to provide assistance with volunteers where needed. The business environment in Samoa changes often, so SWAP provides a central point of connection for those interested in helping the country. Check the website or contact the organization to inquire about current projects connected to sea turtles.

The SWAP headquarters are based at Camp Samoa, a voluntourism center, in Aleisa East and offers four campsites with toilets, showers, and rural Samoan flavor.

More information:
SWAP: swapsamoa.com
Camp Samoa: campsamoa.com

How to help:
Samoans are known as very hospitable and friendly. If you are interested in turtles—or anything Samoan, for that matter—they will enjoy sharing their culture and stories. Make yourself available for short- and long-term volunteer projects here.

⚑ *Arnavons Community Marine Conservation Area, Solomon Islands*

The Arnavons, three large islands that are part of the nearly 1,000-island archipelago known as the Solomon Islands, are one of the Pacific Ocean's most important biodiversity hotspots and a critical sea turtle nesting area. Founded in 1995 through an accord that The Nature Conservancy (TNC) helped broker, the Arnavons Community Marine Conservation Area (ACMCA) is a 40,000-acre MPA run by an unlikely consortium of former poachers and turtle eaters. The Nature Conservancy continues to serve as adviser and works with neighboring communities and governments on conservation plans that steer resource use away from the Arnavons. ACMCA has helped replace lost fishing income by creating fishery centers and sustainable seaweed-harvesting opportunities.

Since formation of the ACMCA, the number of hawksbill turtle nests in the Arnavons has increased, with the number in 2010 double the numbers in the 1990s. New management guidelines included zoning and monitoring protocols to protect and patrol nesting beaches. Three on-site conservation officers—one each from Katupika and Kia, two communities that both claim ownership of the area, and one from Wagina, a community relocated from the Phoenix Islands in Kiribati by the British government in the early 1960s—patrol the waters and lead the sea turtle program. While snorkeling, swimming, or kayaking, visitors to the Arnavons are likely to see hawksbills and may see them nesting on the beach.

People can occasionally visit the project by clearing trips in advance with TNC staff in the Solomons at watu@tnc.org. Because hawksbills nest year-round here, you have a very good chance of seeing a nest emergence. Visitors can also accompany conservation officers on nightly beach patrols on Kerihikapa Island. By staying in the area and using local service providers, you help ensure that these communities can continue to protect their sea turtles.

Turtle Love on the Beach

During the right season on certain beaches, enter the water at your own risk, not because of extreme undertow or heavy shorebreak, poor water quality, red tide, or poisonous jellyfish—although all can present safety concerns. Something entirely different and nearly as dangerous lurks in the water: green turtles in the thick of mating season.

The sight of mating green turtles compels with its grace, beauty, ancient simplicity, and, well, ruggedness. Green turtle mating happens in the water, often beautiful, turquoise tropical water, near idyllic sandy beaches backed by bent palm trees. Add a Barry White soundtrack and a couple of Mai Tais, and it's no wonder the turtles carry on here.

A bit of an aquatic turtle courtship precedes actual mating. Males nip and bump the female. It is similar to watching two boulders with flippers dancing. During the actual act, though, there is little apparent movement other than the female guiding the pair to the surface to breathe. Males hang on to the front edge of the female's shell with a pair of large recurved claws, with another claw at the end of the male's tail creating a sturdy three-point attachment. This is important, as attempts by as many as 17 other males to knock the first male off have been witnessed. Physical damage to both members of the pair is common.

Occasionally, a second male will attach himself to the pair; in fact, as many as four other males have been observed hanging on with, one can only assume, hopeful determination. When this sort of thing happens with 400-pound sea turtles, it's worth a picture.

Male turtles are known to hang in there, so to speak, for up to 12 hours or more. This may well be what led some males of the human species to believe that turtle eggs are aphrodisiacs. Perhaps not surprisingly, dried and shaved green turtle penis is considered similarly potent when added to alcohol. There is no scientific basis that either is particularly effective, and these beliefs, in fact, have contributed greatly to decline in sea turtle populations.

Out in the ocean, though, male sea turtles continue to do their best to go forth and multiply. When things get hot and heavy, the water may be full of males swimming in circles around a female, biting each other, attempting to mate with logs or buoys or, back to that initial warning, you. Male green turtles have been known to get overly friendly with swimmers, snorkelers, or divers. Imagine a big claw on each shoulder and a large tail around underneath, attached to 400 pounds of ready reptile. Consider yourself warned. ■

More information:

The Nature Conservancy Arnavons: http://www.nature.org/ourinitiatives/regions/asiaandthepacific/solomonislands/placesweprotect/arnavon-islands.xml

The Arnavons Islands: arnavons.com

Read the IUCN article about ACMCA: iucn.org/about/work/programmes/gpap_home/pas_gpap/paoftheweek/?11793/Home-for-Hawksbill

Watch *Home for the Hawksbill*, a 29-minute film about how three rival tribes in the Solomons overcame their differences and started working together to save their sea turtles: homeforhawksbill.com/the-film/watch-the-film

How to help:

Make a donation to The Nature Conservancy; $40 buys a tag for a hawksbill, and $200 pays for a week's worth of food for the rangers: support.nature.org/site/Donation2?df_id=9880&9880.donation=form1.

Other things to do in the area:

Papatura Island Retreat. Stay in a bungalow at the retreat, only a few hours away from Arnavons by boat: papatura.com/.

Water sports. Enjoy world-class surfing, snorkeling, and fishing.

Beaches and rain forest. Visit white-sand beaches, and take walks in the rain forests: papatura.com.

Captive Encounters

THIS BOOK contains many stories of how an encounter with a wild sea turtle created a special memory or even changed a life. Nothing compares to seeing an animal up close, in its natural environment, watching it eat, nest, or emerge into this world. We encourage everyone to seek an experience with sea turtles in the wild. When that is not possible, or will not be for some time, observing sea turtles in captivity is the next best thing. This section lists facilities where you can do so.

Sea turtle rehabilitation facilities, hospitals, and educational facilities also play an important role in sea turtle protection and conservation. They create vital opportunities to educate the public and increase awareness. Many people will never have the good fortune to see a sea turtle in the wild, and without places that keep them in captivity, those people would never learn about the importance of these species, the dangers they face, or how we can help.

Not all facilities are created equal, however. We want everyone to be aware of this and to give their support—and admission dollars—only to those that practice good animal husbandry and that put the best interests of individual sea turtles and the species as a whole before anything else. Red flags include profit-making, entertainment-oriented facilities or those that keep sea turtles in crowded or unhealthy conditions or that keep animals that could return to the wild. Private facilities and hotels in Asia, for example, often keep hatchlings in captivity solely for entertainment purposes. Some conduct hatchling releases during the day, which is more convenient for the facility and for tourists but makes it much less likely that the hatchlings will survive.

Ideally, only turtles incapable of surviving on their own should be kept permanently in captivity. Certainly there are exceptions. Sometimes captive turtles contribute to research that will benefit all of their kind. In some cases, a captive sea turtle that could survive in the wild serves an important education and outreach function, perhaps helping to improve conditions for all sea turtles. Most scientists and conservationists can live with a few cases of healthy sea turtles in captivity but worry that a few cases could quickly become many. It is a delicate balance and one that you can play a part in striking.

⛱ *Reef HQ Aquarium, Australia*

The Reef HQ Great Barrier Reef Aquarium in Townsville, Queensland, serves as the national education center for Australia's Great Barrier Reef Marine Park Authority. The Reef HQ Aquarium turtle hospital cares for and rehabilitates sick and injured marine turtles under the C.A.R.E—Conserve. Act. Rehabilitate. Educate—philosophy. It works to raise community awareness of threatened species and encourage behavioral changes that contribute to conservation.

All species of marine turtles found in the Great Barrier Reef Marine Park are listed as threatened by the International Union for the Conservation of Nature and Natural Resources, with the hawksbill turtle listed as critically endangered. Since opening in August 2009, the hospital has released 36 sick and injured marine turtles back into the Great Barrier Reef Marine Park. The Reef HQ Aquarium is open from 9:30 a.m. until 5:00 p.m. 364 days a year (closed Christmas Day). Turtle talks are given at noon and 3:30 p.m. in the Turtle Hospital. An admission ticket allows you to come and go to the facility, and membership includes free admission for a year. 2-68 Flinders Street, +61-7-4750-0800 (international call), reefhq.com.au/

⛱ *Neotropical Foundation, Tenerife, Canary Islands*

This facility rescues and rehabilitates sick and injured sea turtles, releasing to the wild those that become sufficiently healthy. In a typical year, the facility receives 50 to 100 injured turtles and, since its inception in the year 2000, has rehabilitated and released more than 800 sea turtles. The vast majority are loggerheads, with an occasional green or leatherback and, rarely, a hawksbill or olive ridley. The public is invited to many of the releases. Those interested in attending one can send an e-mail to fundacion@neotropico.org and ask to be included on the sea turtle mailing list. Notices of public releases are sent to this list 7 to 10 days in advance, specifying the date, time, and location. Report injured sea turtles to 112, the Canary Islands' emergency phone number. 34-629-123-745 (international call), neotropico.org, fundacion@neotropico.org

Xcaret, Quintana Roo, Mexico

Xcaret, which means "small inlet" in Mayan, is a nature and culture park in the Riviera Maya region of Mexico. Open since 1990, it operates an on-site sea turtle hospital and rehabilitation facility and also supports Flora, Fauna y Cultura's sea turtle conservation and other programs. Xcaret takes in approximately 200 hatchlings from the Flora, Fauna y Cultura project beaches each year, maintaining them for research and education purposes for two years before releasing them. The public can participate in these releases. Xcaret also has a population of adult turtles that are used for monitoring and research. These are on display in natural seawater pools in the park. Carretera Chetumal-Puerto Juárez, Km 282, Playa del Carmen, 1-800-212-8951 (Mexico), 1-888-922-7381 (US and Canada), xcaretexperiencias.com (in Spanish)

South Africa

Two Oceans Aquarium

Located in Cape Town, on the southern tip of the African continent near where the Indian and Atlantic Oceans meet, Two Oceans Aquarium showcases the incredible diversity of marine life found in these oceans. It houses more than 3,000 animals, including sharks, fish, penguins, and sea turtles.

Opened in November 1995, the facility works to raise environmental awareness through exhibits and conservation and education programs, such as the turtle rehabilitation program. Juvenile loggerhead turtles, which hatch on northern beaches, are swept down the coast by the Agulhas Current and washed ashore on beaches off the Cape Peninsula. The aquarium encourages people to bring these turtles to the facility for re-habilitation and eventual release into the Indian Ocean. In both 2011 and 2012, the aquarium released 16 loggerheads, many of which were tagged for scientific research. Dock Road, V&A Waterfront, +27-(0)21-418-3823 (international call), aquarium.co.za

uShaka Marine World

This marine park, which opened in Durban in 2004, includes a Turtle Rehabilitation Center that takes in turtles stranded on the beach or in a rock pool. Loggerhead sea turtles strand the most often, followed by greens and then hawksbills. Often, these turtles hatched on the beaches of northern Kwa-Zulu Natal. They receive initial treatment at Two Oceans Aquarium, then are flown here where water temperatures are warmer to be cared for by qualified rehabilitation staff.

uShaka has an outdoor rehabilitation center specially designed to house young turtles recovering from their trauma at sea, with its own laboratory for weight assessments, minor medical observations, and treatments. Visitors can view turtles throughout the day and watch them being fed and cared for at specific times.

Once the resident veterinarian gives the all-clear, turtles are released into age-appropriate inshore or offshore waters. Generally, turtles are not released until they are at least two years old and thus better equipped to survive. 1 King Shaka Avenue, Point Durban, 27-(0)31-328-8000 (inter-national call), ushakamarineworld.co.za

United States

California, Monterey Bay Aquarium

The mission of the nonprofit Monterey Bay Aquarium, founded in 1984, is to inspire conservation of the oceans, which it does through a variety of collaborations and conservation research projects, including ones on great white sharks and tropical coral propagation.

The Open Sea, the aquarium's largest exhibit, houses tuna, sharks, schools of sardines, and sea turtles—greens and a young loggerhead—

all visible through a 90-foot window. Watch feeding time at 11:00 a.m. daily and a web cam on the Open Sea exhibit from 7:00 a.m. to 7:00 p.m. at montereybayaquarium.org/efc/efc_opensea/open_sea_cam.aspx. 886 Cannery Row, 831-648-4800, montereybayaquarium.com

Florida, Clearwater Marine Aquarium

The Clearwater Marine Aquarium (CMA) includes Turtle Cove, home to Molly, a sea turtle missing both left flippers; Stubby, who is missing both front flippers due to entanglement and is unable to submerge and swim properly; and several other sea turtles. The facility takes in injured and sick sea turtles and cares for them until they are able to be released, but those unlikely to survive in the wild, such as Molly and Stubby, become permanent residents.

The aquarium also monitors almost 26 miles of Pinellas County coastline for nesting activity, sending out early-morning patrols to locate new nesting sites and late-night patrols to check existing nests for hatchlings. Trained volunteers participate in the morning patrols along with staff and interns. Nest sites are marked and GPS coordinates recorded for daily observation.

When it is time for a nest to hatch, it is covered with a nest cage and a volunteer watches it from 10:00 p.m. until 2:00 a.m. The nest cage prevents hatchlings from heading toward bright lights when they emerge. Since 2005, CMA has released more than 60,000 hatchlings into the Gulf of Mexico. Nesting season runs from May to the end of October, with an average of about 120 nests per season. 249 Windward Passage Clearwater, 727-441-1790, seewinter.com

Florida, Loggerhead Marinelife Center of Juno Beach

In addition to offering turtle walks to observe loggerhead nesting March through September (see more information under Florida in the United States section), the center has comprehensive exhibits on sea turtle research, biology, and threats to their survival; area nesting history; and models and skeletons, as well as exhibits on the region's coastal environment. Outside, visitors can get a close look at sick or injured adult and hatchling sea turtles that are being treated at the facility's hospital.

Most are eventually released back into the wild. The property also has picnic pavilions, a nature trail, and beach access and more trails in the adjacent Juno Dunes Natural Area. 14200 US Highway 1, 561-627-8280, marinelife.org

Florida, Mote Marine Laboratory, Sarasota

A Kemp's ridley named Caleb recently joined the Sea Turtles: Ancient Survivors exhibit at the Aquarium at Mote Marine Laboratory. Caleb is the first ridley, but the exhibit also houses loggerhead and green sea turtles that cannot return to the wild. Wildlife officials determined that Caleb should remain in captivity due to impaired swimming ability, and Mote offered to provide the ridley a home. According to Mote's sea turtle care coordinator, Caleb does not have a full range of movement necessary to undergo migration, avoid boats, or escape predators. At the aquarium, this sea turtle will help educate visitors about endangered Kemp's ridleys.

Founded in 1955, Mote Marine Laboratory is an independent, nonprofit organization that conducts marine research through seven research centers and incorporates public outreach as a key part of its mission. In addition to the public aquarium, Mote has a whale and dolphin hospital and a sea turtle hospital that has treated and released more than 100 sea turtles. Volunteer opportunities are available at both of these facilities. Mote also has educational displays about sea turtle conservation and research, including ways the public can help protect wild sea turtles. Individuals can adopt a Mote sea turtle at mote.org/adopt. 1600 Ken Thompson Parkway, 941-388-4441, mote.org

Florida, Sea Turtle Hospital, Marathon Key

Richei Moretti bought a small motel in Marathon, built a new pool, and decided to use the existing saltwater pool as an aquarium. A young guest asked why he had no turtles in the aquarium, and when Moretti investigated, he found there were permits required to keep sea turtles. He decided to rehabilitate sea turtles instead. He purchased an old nightclub next to the hotel and turned it into a hospital with emergency and operating rooms, which appears to have been the first certified sea turtle hospital in the world. The current facility has space for about 50 turtles, and the goal is to rescue, rehabilitate, and release. Releases of recovered turtles are done in public whenever possible, as a way to publicize the need and the work of the hospital. Those that cannot be released due to the nature of their injuries or illnesses are used to promote education about sea turtles.

Tours, offered daily on the hour between 10:00 a.m. and 4:00 p.m., start in a room with exhibits about sea turtles, including their types, nesting, and threats, and on the work of the hospital. Then the operating room and lab are toured, as well as the outdoor tanks occupied by recuperating turtles and permanent residents. A number of impressively sized iguanas lounge around the area as well. 2396 Overseas Highway, 305-743-2552, turtlehospital.org

Georgia Aquarium

The SunTrust Georgia Explorer is an interactive gallery with touch pools of horseshoe crabs and stingrays and several large habitats that feature a loggerhead sea turtle and the fish of Gray's Reef National Marine Sanctuary off the Georgia coast. Georgia Aquarium's 4R Program (Rescue, Rehabilitation, Research, Responsibility) rehabilitates and releases loggerhead sea turtles into the sea.

The Georgia Aquarium recently partnered with The Nature Conservancy (TNC) to save the Arnavon Community Marine Conservation Area (ACMCA) in the Solomon Islands from overfishing. The Solomon Island villagers have become the guardians of these islands, requesting governmental assistance to restore them, protect them from poachers, and monitor the recovery of corals, giant clams, and native fish. In only a few years the recovery of depleted fish and invertebrate species has been dramatic. (Read more about the ACMCA in the South Pacific section.) The Georgia Aquarium has committed itself to fund the ACMCA program for three years. Visitors to the Georgia Aquarium can expect to see more exhibits on and information about this project in the Tropical Diver gallery in late 2013. 225 Baker Street NW, Atlanta, 404-581-4000, georgiaaquarium.org

Georgia Sea Turtle Center, Jekyll Island

Stranded sea turtles are often found along Atlantic coast beaches. Although most are dead, a small but increasing number are still alive. Before the center opened, there were no facilities in Georgia to treat the turtles, so they had to be transported long distances to centers in Florida and South Carolina. Unfortunately, these facilities are often filled to capacity, and the turtles cannot be treated adequately and may be prematurely released.

In February 2006, renovations began on the new Georgia Sea Turtle Center, a marine turtle rehabilitation, research, and education facility on Jekyll Island. The Georgia Sea Turtle Center opened in June 2007 and provided state-of-the-art emergency care to sick and injured sea turtles, with opportunities for scientific research and long-term treatment.

Jekyll Island is an ideal site for the new rehabilitation center. With an active sea turtle monitoring program since 1972, Jekyll is unique among Georgia's developed islands for its significant annual turtle nesting. 214 Stable Road, 912-635-4444, georgiaseaturtlecenter.org

Maryland, National Aquarium, Baltimore

A green sea turtle residing permanently at this aquarium was likely born around 1998. When rescued from Long Island Sound in 2000, she weighed just six pounds, was cold-stunned, and had an infected left front flipper. The flipper had to be amputated, and almost two years later, the turtle was donated to the National Aquarium. At the time, staff believed that she would not survive in the wild minus a flipper, although since then, sea turtles missing all or parts of flippers have been released from rehabilitation facilities. After three months in quarantine, the turtle, nicknamed "Calypso," moved to the Wings in the Water exhibit. Calypso now weighs 490 pounds and lives in the Blacktip Reef exhibit, which replicates Indo-Pacific coral reefs and offers many vantage points, including a floor-to-ceiling pop-out viewing window. 501 E. Pratt Street, 410-576-3800; Stranded Animal Hotline, 410-373-0083; aqua.org

Massachusetts, New England Aquarium, Boston

The New England Aquarium opened in 1969 in Boston and attracts more than 1.3 million visitors each year. In addition, it operates a wide variety of educational programs and conservation initiatives. Groups of up to 10 people can take behind-the-scenes tours, which last about 45 minutes and include a glimpse of the animal care and work of biologists.

Young green sea turtles sometimes spend time in the waters off New England. Inside the aquarium is Myrtle, a green sea turtle approximately 80 years old and weighing more than 500 pounds—a weight she maintains by eating lettuce, cabbage, squid, and brussels sprouts. She has lived at the aquarium since June 1970 and currently resides in the Giant Ocean Tank, a Caribbean coral reef exhibit 23 feet deep and 40 feet wide containing 200,000 gallons of saltwater heated to a prefect 74 tropical degrees. 1 Central Wharf, 617-973-5200, neaq.org/index.php

North Carolina, Karen Beasley Sea Turtle Rescue and Rehabilitation Center, Topsail Beach

A nonprofit staffed by volunteers, this facility cares for sick and injured sea turtles, releasing into the wild those that recover sufficiently. The center also manages patrols on 26 miles of beaches around Topsail for loggerhead nests, mid-May through August. In 2012, some 82 nests were recorded, down slightly from 110 in 2011 and 104 in 2010, but up from 59 in 2009.

The center is open to the public 2:00 to 4:00 p.m. June through August (closed Wednesdays and Sundays). 822 Carolina Avenue, seaturtlehospital.org

The North Carolina Aquariums

The North Carolina Aquariums were established in 1976 to promote an appreciation and conservation of North Carolina's ocean, estuary, river, stream, and other aquatic environments. There are three locations. The one on Roanoke Island has the largest collection of sharks in the state, a display on the waters of the Outer Banks, and an interactive, hands-on exhibit called Operation: Sea Turtle Rescue. A rare white sea turtle lives at the Pine Knoll Shores location; and a loggerhead, in the Let's Talk Turtle exhibit at Fort Fisher.

The North Carolina Wildlife Resources Commission oversees nest and hatchling monitoring conducted by an extensive network of volunteers and institutions, including the North Carolina Aquariums. Weak or disoriented hatchlings come to the aquariums to recuperate, and once they eat and demonstrate healthy activity such as diving, most are released offshore.

Some remain at the aquarium for use in exhibits and programs to educate the public for one to four years before release. Many of these are outfitted with satellite transmitters to help scientists learn more about the movements and habits of sea turtles.

All three aquariums respond to sea turtle strandings; the facility on Roanoke Island houses the Network for Endangered Sea Turtles Rehabilitation Facility, and those at Pine Knoll Shores and Fort Fisher take in turtles in need of rehabilitation when additional space is needed. Roanoke Island, 374 Airport Road, Manteo; Pine Knoll Shores, 1 Roosevelt Blvd; Fort Fisher, 900 Loggerhead Road, Kure Beach; 800-832-3474, ncaquariums.com

South Carolina Aquarium Sea Turtle Hospital, Charleston

The stated mission of this nonprofit organization is to inspire "conservation of the natural world by exhibiting and caring for animals, by excelling in education and research, and by providing an exceptional visitor experience." It aids sick and injured sea turtles through a Sea Turtle Rescue Program; the South Carolina Department of Natural Resources (SCDNR) brings sick and injured sea turtles found along the coast to the aquarium's Turtle Hospital, where animal care staff monitor and treat the animal. On average, a sea turtle stays in rehabilitation for seven to eight months and, once deemed healthy enough to survive on its own, is released on a local beach.

Behind-the-scenes tours of the hospital are offered on Monday, Wednesday, Friday, Saturday, and Sunday at 11:30 a.m. and 1:00 p.m. Call 843-577-FISH for reservations. Individuals can also make a donation or adopt a turtle. To report a sick or injured sea turtle, contact the local police department or call the SCDNR hotline, 800-922-5431.

A 220-pound-plus loggerhead also lives in a two-story, 385,000-gallon Great Ocean Tank, part of the Ocean Gallery, an exhibit on the ocean habitats off the coast of South Carolina. 100 Aquarium Wharf, Charleston, 843-720-1990, scaquarium.org

Texas, NOAA Fisheries Galveston Laboratory

Part of the National Oceanic and Atmospheric Administration's National Marine Fisheries Service, the Southeast Fisheries Science Center in Galveston conducts research on turtle excluder devices (TEDs) and other fishing gear, seeking to identify ways to reduce sea turtle bycatch. Researchers bring several hundred loggerhead hatchlings to the center each year from Florida. While they grow large enough to participate in TED research, the turtles sometimes contribute to other studies and graduate student work. Two-year-old turtles are used in the TED research and then released back into their native Florida waters.

The center used to be open to the public on a regular basis, but extensive repairs and cleanup necessary after Hurricane Ike and, later, a shortage of staff made it too hard to maintain that schedule. Now, trained and knowledgeable volunteers conduct tours of the facility when there is enough demand. You will see the main building where the three classes of hatchlings are kept—those from the current year, one-year-olds, and two-year-olds that have yet to complete their TED work. You also get a look at the facility's turtle hospital, which rescues and rehabilitates stranded turtles from the northern Texas coast. The hospital encourages anyone who finds a turtle onshore or catches one while fishing—even if it seems to be fine—to call. Sometimes turtles caught by fishers have been caught before and may have multiple hooks inside their bodies. Despite rumors to the contrary, sea turtle's stomachs do not dissolve these hooks; they must be removed. The number to call (anywhere in Texas) is 866-TURTLE-5. 4600 Avenue U, 409-766-3500 (call ahead to schedule a visit), www.galvestonlab.sefsc.noaa.gov

Texas, Sea Turtle Inc., South Padre Island

This facility treats sick and injured turtles, releasing those capable of surviving in the wild and giving the others a permanent home here or at another zoological facility. These nonreleasable individuals give the public a chance to see turtles up close through daily informational shows and turtle feeding and touching. One of most famous is Allison, a green sea turtle with only one flipper, the rest probably lost in a shark attack. There was not enough left of any of her lost flippers to hold a prosthetic device. Unable to do anything but swim in circles, Allison seemed doomed to a short and unhappy life. Then one of Sea Turtle Inc.'s (STI) summer interns, 21-year-old Tom Wilson, had an idea. Applying the physics of canoe paddling, Wilson and scientists worked out equations and developed a turtle wet suit that covers about half of Allison's body. A dorsal fin, adapted from a wind surfboard, acts like a rudder, and carefully placed weights give her stability.

"With the suit on, in the water, she is transformed," says Jeff George, curator at STI. "She acts like a normal turtle. She swims, dives, surfaces to breathe, and even nips at other turtles."

In addition to live turtles, Sea Turtle Inc. has displays on turtle biology, nesting, and hazards and a gift shop featuring turtle merchandise. Much of it provides income to those who live near nesting beaches. For example, a line of ceramics produced by residents near the Mexican nesting beaches helps fund ongoing protection of nesting turtles. These ceramics are also sold at the Texas State Aquarium and Brownsville's Gladys Porter Zoo. 6617 Padre Blvd, 956-761-4511, seaturtleinc.org

Texas A&M University at Galveston Sea Life Facility

Texas A&M University at Galveston's campus on Pelican Island includes a research laboratory and rehabilitation facility. Turtles from the NOAA hospital are often brought here to grow and get stronger prior to their release. A small Outreach Center open to the public has large windows overlooking the lab's main room and several tanks where rehabilitating sea turtles swim. The rest of the tanks can be viewed via a monitor on the wall that live-streams from cameras above each (the tank cams can be watched online as well). Wall panels provide information about sea turtles and threats to their survival, a sea turtle skeleton hangs from the ceiling, and visitors can check out items related to specific animals in the facility, such as a weathered tennis shoe that had entangled a sea turtle. There is a picnic area outside, and special T-shirts sold in the bookstore next door help fund sea turtle food. When the facility releases a turtle onshore, the public is invited (check the website for release dates). 200 Seawolf Parkway, 409-740-4574, tamug.edu/sealife/

Texas State Aquarium, Corpus Christi

The Texas State Aquarium looks out on Corpus Christi Bay and, beyond, the Gulf of Mexico. Outside, it features a boardwalk over a small wetland exhibit, where visitors can experience firsthand the wash of waves and feel of the wind. Inside, the three-story facility showcases more than 300 species, mostly from the waters of the Gulf of Mexico and including an offshore rig and Flower Gardens exhibits, jellyfish tanks, dolphin shows, sea otters, and rescued sea turtles. These turtles, which cannot be returned to the wild, occupy a large tank with several viewing windows on its side and a platform for looking into it from the top. Visitors can observe scheduled feedings. 2710 N. Shoreline Blvd, 361-881-1200, texasstateaquarium.org

Virginia Aquarium and Marine Science Center

The Virginia Aquarium houses hands-on exhibits; an outdoor aviary, nature trail, and marshlands; and more than 800,000 gallons of live animal habitats. The facility also rescues, rehabilitates, and releases stranded sea turtles. You can see a list of "patients" and check their current status at virginiaaquarium.com/research-conservation/Pages/recent-rescues.aspx. Also, each year, four loggerhead hatchlings from nests at Back Bay National Wildlife Refuge and False Cape State Park are brought to the Virginia Aquarium and Marine Science Center for study, display, and eventual release, through a partnership with the US Fish and Wildlife Service, Back Bay National Wildlife Refuge, and Virginia Department of Game and Inland Fisheries.

They spend one year here, while animal care staff collect data that will help us better understand the early growth and development of loggerheads. The turtles are released off the coasts of Virginia and North Carolina into *Sargassum* mats in the Gulf Stream, where their fellow hatchlings are believed to spend much of their early years at sea. Some of them are now equipped with satellite transmitters so scientists can monitor their movements and behavior in the ocean.

Loggerhead, Kemp's ridley, and green sea turtles live in the facility's Light Tower Aquarium, designed to simulate the area around the Chesapeake Bay Light Tower. The turtles share the facility with a variety of fish, including Atlantic spadefish, a large goliath grouper, triple tail, cobia, lookdown fish, and permits.

During a 45-minute Behind the Scenes Experience you can get a look at resident sea turtles from the top of their aquarium, observe feeding, learn about the care of these animals, and hear about the history and behavior of sea turtles and conservation efforts worldwide. Tours are held Monday, Wednesday, and Friday at 1:00 p.m. 717 General Booth Blvd., Virginia Beach, 757-385-3474, virginiaaquarium.com

Controversy in the Caymans

SEA TURTLES loom large in the history of the Caymans, three islands south of Cuba and northwest of Jamaica. European explorers in the 1600s wrote of seeing these animals in such great numbers that it seemed as if one could walk across the sea on their backs. Sailing ships began to rely on this abundance as provision for their voyages, and a sea turtle fishery established in the islands thrived for decades.

This unsustainable harvest of slow-to-mature and easy-to-catch sea turtles took its toll, and by the mid-1800s, numbers had fallen so drastically that some sea turtle fishers left for islands south of Cuba and for Nicaragua. The International Union for Conservation of Nature (IUCN) declared that the Cayman Islands' green sea turtle population was extinct by 1900. Today, the Department of Environment reports that fewer than 30 greens nest in the Cayman Islands each year.

The Cayman Turtle Farm (CTF) was established on Grand Cayman by a group of US and UK investors in 1968 to provide a reliable supply of sea turtles for products and food, especially sea turtle soup, a popular dish in the islands. The founders went bankrupt in 1975, and new owners took over. Those owners also failed, however, and in 1983, the Cayman government took ownership and began operating the farm as a private company. After a hurricane in 2001, the facility moved farther inland and added more tourist elements. It became one of the largest land-based tourist attractions in the Caymans, visited by hundreds of thousands of people each year, many of them from cruise ships. It educates and informs the public about sea turtles, and its operators say that raising the animals to produce products helps protect wild sea turtles from poaching. The farm claims to have obtained all its wild turtles and eggs legally, with the last breeding turtles bought in 1975 and the last eggs collected in 1976.

There is, however, evidence that the farm did not, in fact, receive its original egg and live stock legally, but illegally from Costa Rica. Further, several conservation groups counter that the farm simply keeps demand alive for turtle products and that it serves to condone the concept of using sea turtles for human consumption.

The farm points to its releases of sea turtles into the wild each year as helping to replenish the local population. Since 1968, it has released 35,000 turtles—including 40 hatchlings in 2011 and 150 yearlings and hatchlings in 2012—although only 11 are known to have returned to nest on the island.

But the Sea Turtle Conservancy objects to the CTF's release of captive-raised turtles into the wild on the basis of the potential to affect wild populations in the broader Caribbean. Such release could spread diseases that are found primarily in captive turtles to wild populations (officials at the facility say turtles are quarantined and reviewed prior to release). In addition, STC says that the farm's breeding turtles come from many nesting colonies so have very different genetics, which means that interbreeding between them and wild sea turtles could affect navigation abilities and genetics. Finally, the release program creates the false impression that we can conserve wild sea turtles simply by breeding them in tanks and releasing them.

David Godfrey, Sea Turtle Conservancy executive director, points out that despite a lack of evidence that the release program benefits the wild population, people around the world are led to believe that the program is a successful option for saving and restoring wild sea turtle numbers.

The World Society for the Protection of Animals (WSPA) conducted an undercover operation in 2012, producing video footage revealing dirty, overcrowded enclosures, conditions ripe for the spread of disease. The crowded conditions often resulted in cannibalism among the turtles, WSPA investigators reported, noting numerous turtles had flippers chewed off by other turtles. In the fall of 2012, some 300 turtles died at the farm after a pipe bringing in seawater malfunctioned.

The WSPA also objects to the practice of allowing visitors to handle sea turtles at the farm. Handling not only stresses these animals but can also cause injury because people sometimes drop them. A recent study suggests that handling can be unsafe for the humans as well, putting them at risk of *Vibrio* infections. WSPA also says that visitors to the farm may not be aware that most of the animals are raised for food; according to a survey taken between 2010 and 2012, some 89 percent of cruise passengers said they were not made aware that the farm breeds turtles for human consumption. Eighty-five percent said they would not have handled the turtles if they had known it distressed the animals.

Public opinion can be a powerful thing and has often been responsible for positive social change. Where society once viewed animals as existing solely for our use and pleasure, that kind of thinking has largely disappeared. Instead, more and more people recognize the value of wild animals and natural habitat for its own sake, for the beauty and pleasure they create, and for the valuable economic services that natural systems provide, including water purification, improved air quality, and storm absorption. Sea turtles serve valuable ecosystem functions around the world. But they also are ancient inhabitants of this planet, graceful and resilient. Perhaps it is time we question using them for our own gain. ■

Resources and Organizations

SEA TURTLES perhaps have inspired more organizations and projects than any other wild animal. This section lists many but certainly not all organizations that provide information about sea turtles or work toward their protection and conservation, whether in the wild, in classrooms, or in the halls of government buildings. The listing is simply alphabetical, with a brief description of the organization and a web address, if available, or other contact information.

ARCAS. Asociación de Rescate y Conservación de Vida Silvestre, a Guatemalan nonprofit wildlife conservation, rescue, and advocacy organization that runs a rescue and rehabilitation center; conducts public and environmental education; and carries out sea turtle, mangrove, and community development projects on the country's Pacific coast: arcasguatemala.com.

ARCHELON. The Sea Turtle Protection Society of Greece, a nonprofit NGO that protects sea turtles and habitat in Greece: archelon.gr./eng/volunt.php?row=row2.

ASTOP. Save the Turtles of Parismina is a community-based project protecting turtles and nesting beaches in the Costa Rican community of Parismina: parisminaturtles.org.

Baja California Association for the Protection of the Environment and the Marine Turtle. Known as ASUPMATOMA in Spanish, this organization coordinates sea turtle conservation and education efforts in the Los Cabos area: asupmatoma.org (in Spanish).

BLUEMIND. An organization that links neuroscience with nature in the new field of neuroconservation. The benefits extend to public health, business, coastal planning, travel, real estate, and rebuilding an emotional connection with water. It provides deeper insights into the science of "our brains on water" and expands the ecosystem services concept to include the vast array of cognitive value offered by healthy waterways. The group holds an annual summit bringing together top neuroscientists, oceanographers, explorers, educators, and artists: bluemind.me.

California Academy of Sciences. A scientific institution "committed to leading-edge research, educational outreach, and finding new and innovative ways to engage and inspire the public." Founded in 1853 to conduct natural science research, the academy currently has a research group of about 100 people, including curator scientists, collections managers, postdoctoral researchers, students, and a network of accomplished research associates working around the world: calacademy.org.

Cotorco. The Committee for the Conversation of the Sea Turtles of Corcovado is a community organization that operates a sea turtle conservation program and hatchery on Costa Rica's Osa Peninsula: cotorco.org/english.

Dakshin Foundation. A nonprofit NGO registered as a charitable trust in India to advocate conservation and natural resource management and support "sustainable livelihoods, social development, and environmental justice." Promotes ecologically and socially appropriate approaches to conservation and management in India's coastal, marine, and mountain ecosystems: dakshin.org.

The Dominica Sea Turtle Conservation Organization. Promotes connections between science, policy, and public participation in sea turtle research, conservation, and education in the Commonwealth of Dominica, with a focus on community involvement. Works with a variety of organizations, agencies, and businesses, including WIDECAST: 767-275-0724, 767-448-4091, domsetco@gmail.com.

Eastern Pacific Hawksbill Initiative. Known by its Spanish acronym, ICAPO, the group collaborates with local communities, scientists, and policy makers in the region to protect hawksbills along the Pacific coast of the Americas, a population some researchers believe is the most endangered in the world: hawksbill.org.

Global Sea Turtle Network. An international network founded to support research and conservation efforts in the sea turtle community, primarily through a website that includes a definitive list of resources on the web, a sea turtle news archive, and an online home and logistic support for other sea turtle organizations. It also provides online access to the *Marine Turtle Newsletter/Noticiero de Tortugas Marinas*, supports registration and administration of the Annual Symposium on Sea Turtle Biology and Conservation, and provides information and support for conservation efforts related to the Inter-American Convention for the Protection and Conservation of Sea Turtles and X'cacel, Mexico: seaturtle.org.

Grupo Tortuguero. A grassroots network in Baja California, Mexico, that conducts sea turtle monitoring and nesting beach conservation, stranding assessment, fishing bycatch reduction, and research: facebook.com/grupo.tortuguero (in Spanish).

International Dark Sky Association. This education organization, based in Arizona, seeks to preserve our natural night sky, recognizing that light pollution threatens astronomy facilities, ecologically sensitive habitats, energy use, and wildlife. It provides expert advice and technology for wildlife-friendly lighting, including ways to protect nesting and hatchling sea turtles: darksky.org.

International Union for Conservation of Nature Red List of Threatened Species. Worldwide listing of vulnerable, endangered, and critically endangered species: iucnredlist.org.

Karumbé. This Uruguayan nonprofit organization, whose name means "turtle" in the Guarani language, has a sea turtle project working with juvenile green sea turtles and with stranded loggerhead, leatherback, and hawksbill turtles. The organization also monitors local artisanal fisheries and collects bycatch data: karumbe.org, facebook.com/karumbe.org.

Leatherback Trust. A nonprofit foundation established by James R. Spotila. Leatherback Trust scientists were instrumental in founding a new national park, Parque Marino Las Baulas, on the Pacific coast of Costa Rica, which protects one of the most important leatherback nesting beaches in the eastern Pacific Ocean. These scientists also train park rangers and guides, work with local schoolchildren, and advise the local community on living in harmony with leatherbacks: leatherback.org.

Leatherback Watch. This citizen science project "collaborates with charter vessels, research expeditions, and local yacht clubs to compile, record, and communicate . . . sightings of leatherback sea turtles off the coasts of California, Oregon, and Washington." The program shares its data with the global scientific community through OBIS-SEAMAP and SIMoN, the Sanctuary Integrated Monitoring Network: seaturtles .org/article.php?id=2032.

MEDASSET. The Mediterranean Association to Save the Sea Turtles, registered in the UK, protects sea turtles and their habitats throughout the Mediterranean through research programs, campaigns, education, and political lobbying: medasset.org.

Mission Blue. An initiative of the Sylvia Earle Alliance, a 501(c)(3) organization formed after Earle was awarded the 2009 TED Prize. It operates as a hub of more than 100 conservation groups, corporations, scientists, and individuals that seeks to elevate public awareness about ocean issues and inspire support for those working to make a difference on those issues: mission-blue.org/.

National Oceanic and Atmospheric Administration Fisheries Office of Protected Resources. Provides information on US government rules, regulations, and protections relating to sea turtle species: www.nmfs. noaa.gov/pr/species/turtles/.

The Nature Conservancy. Founded in 1951 to conserve the lands and waters on which all life depends, this organization works through a staff of more than 550 scientists located in all 50 US states and 35 countries. It partners with individuals, governments, local nonprofit organizations, and corporations to advance conservation around the world and has a number of projects related to sea turtles: nature.org.

Ningaloo Turtle Program. A program developed by the Cape Conservation Group, Department of Environment and Conservation, Murdoch University, and World Wildlife Fund–Australia that contributes to the conservation of marine turtles and their associated habitats in Australia: ningalooturtles.org.au.

North Carolina Sea Turtle Project. Run by the North Carolina Wildlife Resources Commission, Division of Wildlife Management, to monitor nesting and strandings along the North Carolina coast: seaturtle.org/ groups/ncwrc/overview.html.

Ocean Conservancy. A nonprofit organization that works to keep the oceans healthy through advocacy, research, and education: oceanconservancy.org.

Ocean Foundation. A community foundation to support, strengthen, and promote organizations "dedicated to reversing the trend of destruction of ocean environments around the world," by growing the financial resources available to support marine conservation and promote healthy ocean ecosystems: oceanfdn.org/.

Ocean Positive. A California-based nonprofit organization using a community-based approach to protect the Coral Triangle, bordered by the Philippines, eastern Indonesia, and the Solomon Islands. One of its projects is collaborative research on leatherback sea turtles in West Papua, Indonesia, and it plans to train local Papuans to help save these gigantic and majestic animals: oceanpositive.org.

Ocean Spirits. A nonprofit organization founded in Granada in 1999 to protect that country's sea turtles through research, education, and development of sustainable ecotourism: oceanspirits.org.

Osa Conservation. This nonprofit organization operates a sea turtle conservation program on Piro and Pejeperro beaches south of Corcovado National Park in Costa Rica: osaconservation.org.

Pacific Marine Resources Institute. A nonprofit organization based on Saipan in the northern Mariana Islands, dedicated to "working in partnership with Pacific nations, states, and communities to assess, monitor, and manage . . . biological resources for sustainable use": pacmares.com/Home.html.

PRETOMA. Programa Restauración de Tiburones y Tortugas Marinas is a marine conservation and research NGO that runs sea turtle and shark conservation projects in Costa Rica: pretoma.org.

Projeto TAMAR. The Chico Mendes Institute for Biodiversity Conservation, an agency of the Ministry of Environment, and the Foundation Pro-Tamar have conducted research, protection, and management of sea turtles in Brazil for 33 years. The organization protects about 1,100 miles of beaches through 23 research bases: tamar.org.br.

RED Sustainable Travel. Supports local residents throughout northwestern Mexico, with training and business assistance, working to create tourism opportunities out of conservation efforts: redtravelmexico.com.

Samoa Web Ambassadors Programme. A Samoan charitable trust established to teach marketing in Samoa and to encourage in-bound Samoan tourism: swapsamoa.com.

Save Our Sea Turtles. Manages a community-based leatherback and hawksbill sea turtle project in Tobago in partnership with WIDE-CAST and the Turtle Village Trust: sos-tobago.org, facebook.com/SOSTobago, info@sos-tobago.org.

SeaGrass Grow! A program from the Ocean Foundation offering greenhouse gas emission offset in the ocean—known as "Blue Carbon." Includes a Blue Carbon Offset Calculator that allows you to calculate annual carbon dioxide (CO_2) emissions from an individual, family, company, or organization and the amount of Blue Carbon necessary to fully or partially offset those emissions (acres of seagrass to be restored or equivalent): seagrassgrow.org.

Sea Turtle Conservancy. Established as the Caribbean Conservation Corporation in 1959 by Archie Carr, this is the world's oldest sea turtle research and conservation group. An international nonprofit 501(c)(3) organization headquartered in Florida, it conducts programs to conserve and recover sea turtle populations through research, education, advocacy, and protection of natural habitats worldwide: conserveturtles.org.

Sea Turtle Foundation. A nonprofit NGO in Australia that protects and conserves sea turtles through research, education, advocacy, and other actions, including stranding response and lighting projects: seaturtlefoundation.org.

Sea Turtles Forever. A nonprofit organization based in Oregon that runs a Sea Turtle Hotline for reporting sea turtle sightings in northeastern Pacific foraging areas (503-739-1446), the Oregon Marine Micro-Plastic Response Team in the United States, and the Punta Pargos Green Turtle Monitoring and Protection Program and Lagartillo Reef Monofilament and Marine Plastic Debris Survey in Costa Rica: seaturtlesforever.com.

Sea Turtles of India. A website with information about sea turtle research and conservation projects, as well as resources, including the Turtle Action Group, "a network of NGOs and local and community-based organisations dedicated to the cause of sea turtle conservation and coastal protection in India, including the mainland, Andaman [and] Nicobar Islands, and Lakshadweep [Island]." The website is maintained by the Dakshin Foundation, Bangalore, with funding support from the Marine Turtle Conservation Fund of the US Fish and Wildlife Service and administrative support from the Centre for Herpetology/Madras Crocodile Bank Trust, Mamallapuram: seaturtlesofindia.org.

Sea Turtles of the Mariana Islands. A website about sea turtles and efforts to protect them in the US Commonwealth of the Northern Mariana Islands: ihaggan.com/Welcome.html.

Sea Turtle Restoration Project. A nonprofit organization based in California that works to protect and restore endangered sea turtles and marine biodiversity worldwide through education and advocacy. Part of the Turtle Island Restoration Network: seaturtles.org.

SEEturtles. Founded in 2008 to protect endangered sea turtles through conservation travel and educational programs. One of its initiatives, Billion Baby Turtles, supports efforts to save hatchlings at important nesting beaches around the world, with every dollar donated helping to protect at least one baby turtle: seeturtles.org.

SEEtheWild. The world's first online wildlife conservation travel directory, supporting conservation of wildlife by promoting alternatives to destructive activities and offering ways for travelers to directly support conservation projects. Every trip benefits wildlife conservation programs and communities: seethewild.org.

SOS Tartarugas. Founded in Sal, Cape Verde, Africa, in 2007 by Juan Blanco and Jacquie Cozens in an effort to stop the slaughter of sea turtles on the island. The NGO partners with the Cabo Verdean government and collaborates with the Ministry of Environment, local government, Fisheries Department, other conservation organizations, and law enforcement agencies. During nesting season, it hires Turtle Rangers to patrol beaches and maintain a hatchery: sostartarugas. org/SOSTartarugas/Welcome.html.

South Carolina Marine Turtle Conservation Program. The state's Wildlife and Freshwater Fisheries Division, Department of Natural Resources, works with volunteers, researchers, and biologists from various agencies. The program is involved with nest protection and monitoring and strandings: dnr.sc.gov/seaturtle/.

Turtle Foundation. An international charitable organization with offices in the United States, Germany, Switzerland, and Indonesia dedicated to volunteer efforts that currently operates protection projects in Indonesia and Boa Vista, Cape Verde, Africa: turtle-foundation.org.

TurtleSafe Flashlights. Founded by an outdoorsman and former Jekyll Island lifeguard, this company produces a rechargeable, red LED flashlight that has been tested as safe to use around nesting turtles. The lights can be purchased online: turtlesafeonline.com.

WIDECAST. The Wider Caribbean Sea Turtle Conservation Network is an international scientific network of more than 60 coordinators in more than 40 Caribbean nations and territories, working with a coalition of scientists, managers, conservationists, policy makers, educators, and others in government and nongovernment positions to bring the best available science to bear on management and conservation of sea turtles. Develops and replicates pilot projects; provides technical assistance; links science, policy, and public participation; and enables coordination of the collection, sharing, and use of information and data. It works closely with local communities and managers: widecast .org.

Wildlife Conservation Society. Founded in 1895 to save wildlife and wild places across the globe, this organization currently manages about 500 conservation projects in more than 60 countries and educates millions of visitors at five institutions in New York City: the Bronx Zoo, New York Aquarium, Central Park Zoo, Prospect Park Zoo, and Queens Zoo: wcs.org.

Wildlife Protection Society of India. Provides support and information to government authorities to combat poaching and illegal wildlife trade, deals with human-animal conflicts, and provides support for research projects. One of its projects, Operation Kachhapa, helps conserve olive ridley sea turtles in the Orissa region: wpsi-india.org/wpsi/ index.php.

World Wildlife Fund. Founded in April 1961, WWF is now the world's largest independent conservation organization working on more than 12,000 conservation initiatives to bring a balance between human demands on the world and its wildlife. Marine turtles are one of the organization's priority species: wwf.panda.org.

Yayasan Pulau Banyak. An NGO that protects Pulau Bangkaru, Indonesia's main nesting site, from egg poaching and raises awareness in the area regarding environmental issues: acehturtleconservation.org.

Index